NEW YORK
YANKEE
RECORDS

John A. Mercurio

Also by John A. Mercurio

Major League Baseball Records
Official Profiles of Baseball Hall of Famers
Babe Ruth's Incredible Records
Boston Red Sox Records

NEW YORK YANKEE
RECORDS

JOHN A. MERCURIO

A division of Shapolsky Publishers, Inc.

New York Yankees Records

S.P.I. BOOKS
A division of Shapolsky Publishers, Inc.

Copyright © 1989, 1993 by John A. Mercurio

Previously printed by Harper & Row, Publishers, NY as
Chronology of New York Yankee Records

ISBN 1-56171-215-9

For any additional information, contact:

S.P.I. BOOKS/Shapolsky Publishers, Inc.
136 West 22nd Street
New York, NY 10011
212/633-2022 / FAX 212/633-2123

Printed in Canada

10 9 8 7 6 5 4 3 2 1

To Christopher

CONTENTS

PREFACE

The New York Yankees have had one of the proudest traditions of any team in the history of American sports. They have been the most successful baseball franchise and have won more pennants (33) and World Series (22) than any other team by far. In doing so, they have compiled the most wins (7,596), the highest winning percentage (.567), the most home runs (10,036), the highest batting average (.271—tied with Detroit), the highest slugging percentage (.393), the lowest ERA (3.42), and the most saves (1,967), and they are tied for the highest fielding percentage with .971. (These figures include the 1901 and 1902 seasons, when New York took over the Baltimore franchise.) But what is most amazing about the accomplishments of the New York Yankees is that they are number one in all the major categories, and these include the statistics that start in 1876, the first year of Major League baseball. This means that many of the National League teams had a 24-year head start, and yet the New York Yankees have caught up with and passed all of them!

The Yankees have had perhaps more great players than any other team. From the "Murderers' Row" of the 1920s to Casey Stengel's world-championship teams of the 1950s right up to today's teams with Don Mattingly, Dave Winfield, Ron Guidry, Rickey Henderson, and Dave Righetti, the Yankees have always had a tradition of great record-breaking achievements. It is this book's intent to set forth the batting, pitching, fielding, rookie, and managing records

as they were set and broken over the course of the years.

New York took over the Baltimore franchise in 1903, and the team was first known as the Highlanders because its ballpark was located in Washington Heights, on the highest tract of land in Manhattan Island. The name was never popular, and gradually the name was changed to the Yankees by 1913.

This book consists of chronological lists that begin with the first record holder, in the year 1903, and shows each and every subsequent record holder up to the present. A sample, the season home run record, would look like this:

Most Home Runs

1903	Herm McFarland	5
1904	John Ganzel	6
1912	Guy Zinn	6
1916	Wally Pipp	12
1920	Babe Ruth	**54
1921	Babe Ruth	**59
1927	Babe Ruth	**60
1961	**Roger Maris**	***61

The above is the complete history of the Yankee season home run record. Herm McFarland led his 1903 team with five home runs, a record that lasted only one year, as John Ganzel hit six in 1904. Guy Zinn tied this mark eight years later, and Wally Pipp became the

* Indicates an American League record.
** Indicates a Major League record.
*** Indicates an unbroken Major League record.

first Yankee to hit a dozen homers. Babe Ruth dominated the home run record and set three separate records from 1920 to 1927. He remained the king until 1961, when Roger Maris did what most experts said would never happen.

In this case Roger Maris's record is not only a Yankee record but also a Major League record, as were Babe Ruth's before him. In order to see who holds or held these records for all time, see also my book *Chronology of Major League Baseball Records.*

CHRONOLOGY OF NEW YORK YANKEE RECORDS

CHAPTER 1

SEASON BATTING RECORDS

BATTING QUIZ

1. The Yankee record for most at bats is 692. Who holds it?
2. This super Yankee holds the record for most doubles and most hits. Name him.
3. What Yankee came the closest to hitting .400?
4. Can you name the Yankee who struck out the most times in one season?
5. Whose record for longest Yankee hitting streak did Joe DiMaggio break?

DID YOU KNOW that Johnny Mize's pinch at bats record has not been broken in 35 years?

DID YOU KNOW that Babe Ruth has seven unbroken Yankee season batting records?

DID YOU KNOW that when Don Mattingly belted 238 hits in 1986 he broke a 59-year-old record held by Earle Combs?

YOGI BERRA, BOB TURLEY, MICKEY MANTLE

BABE RUTH
*A young Lou Gehrig receives a tip from the great Bambino.
Will anybody ever break the Babe's slugging mark?*

BABE RUTH
*He was the greatest of them all. For the first time, the records shown on these pages
magnify his greatness.*

THE GREAT JOE DIMAGGIO

Most Games

1903	Jimmy Williams	132
	Willie Keeler	132
1904	Jimmy Williams	146
1905	Willie Keeler	149
1906	Willie Keeler	**152
1914	Roger Peckinpaugh	**157
1937	Lou Gehrig	**157
1938	Lou Gehrig	**157
1961	**Bobby Richardson**	**162
1970	**Roy White**	**162
1973	**Roy White**	**162
1978	**Chris Chambliss**	162
1986	**Don Mattingly**	162

Most At Bats

1903	Willie Keeler	515
1904	Jimmy Williams	559
1905	Willie Keeler	560
1906	Hal Chase	597
1920	Wally Pipp	610
1923	Joe Dugan	644
1927	Earle Combs	648
1937	Red Rolfe	648
1939	Frank Crosetti	656
1961	Bobby Richardson	662
1962	**Bobby Richardson**	692

Most Hits

1903	Willie Keeler	164
1904	Willie Keeler	186
1906	Hal Chase	193
1921	Babe Ruth	204
1923	Babe Ruth	205
1927	Earle Combs	231
1986	**Don Mattingly**	238

Most Singles

1903	Willie Keeler	143
1904	Willie Keeler	*162
1906	**Willie Keeler**	*166
1927	**Earle Combs**	*166

Most Doubles

1903	Jimmy Williams	30
1904	Jimmy Williams	31
1911	Hal Chase	32
1920	Aaron Ward	40
	Bob Meusel	40
1921	Babe Ruth	44
1923	Babe Ruth	45
1926	Lou Gehrig	47
1927	Lou Gehrig	52
1986	**Don Mattingly**	53

Most Triples

1903	Wid Conroy	12
	Jimmy Williams	12
1904	Wid Conroy	12
1907	Jimmy Williams	13
1909	Birdie Cree	16
1910	Birdie Cree	16
1911	Birdie Cree	22
1927	**Earle Combs**	23

Most Home Runs

1903	Herm McFarland	5
1904	John Ganzel	6
1912	Guy Zinn	6
1916	Wally Pipp	12
1920	Babe Ruth	**54
1921	Babe Ruth	**59
1927	Babe Ruth	**60
1961	**Roger Maris**	***61

Highest Home Run Percentage

1903	Herm McFarland	1.4
1912	Guy Zinn	1.5
1916	Frank Baker	2.8
1920	**Babe Ruth**	***11.8

Most Extra Base Hits

1903	Jimmy Williams	45
1911	Birdie Cree	56
1920	Babe Ruth	**99
1921	**Babe Ruth**	***119

---

* American League Record
** Major League Record
*** Unbroken Major League Record

Casey Stengel on Yogi Berra: "He's a man who looks funny in a baseball uniform."

Most Total Bases

1903	Jimmy Williams	197
1904	Willie Keeler	222
1906	Hal Chase	236
1911	Birdie Cree	263
1920	Babe Ruth	388
1921	**Babe Ruth**	***457

Highest Batting Average

1903	Willie Keeler	.318
1904	Willie Keeler	.343
1911	Birdie Cree	.348
1920	Babe Ruth	.376
1921	Babe Ruth	.378
1923	**Babe Ruth**	.393

Highest Slugging Percentage

1903	Jimmy Williams	.392
1904	Willie Keeler	.409
1910	Birdie Cree	.422
1911	Birdie Cree	.513
1920	**Babe Ruth**	***.847

Most Runs Scored

1903	Willie Keeler	95
1906	Willie Keeler	96
1920	Babe Ruth	*158
1921	**Babe Ruth**	*177

Most RBIs

1903	Jimmy Williams	82
1904	John Anderson	82
1906	Hal Chase	84
1911	Roy Hartzell	91
1916	Wally Pipp	93
1920	Babe Ruth	137
1921	Babe Ruth	**171
1927	Lou Gehrig	**175
1931	**Lou Gehrig**	*184

Most Bases on Balls

1903	Lefty Davis	43
1904	Wid Conroy	43
1905	Jimmy Williams	50
1908	Charlie Hemphill	59
1910	Harry Wolter	66
1913	Harry Wolter	80
1920	Babe Ruth	**148
1923	**Babe Ruth**	***170

Most Strikeouts

1903–12	Statistics Not Kept	
1913	Birdie Cree	51
1914	Roger Peckinpaugh	73
1915	Wally Pipp	81
1916	Wally Pipp	82
1921	Bob Meusel	88
1923	Babe Ruth	93
1926	Tony Lazzeri	96
1937	Frank Crosetti	105
1952	Mickey Mantle	111
1958	Mickey Mantle	120
1959	Mickey Mantle	126
1975	**Bobby Bonds**	137

Most Stolen Bases

1903	Wid Conroy	33
1905	Dave Fultz	44
1911	Birdie Cree	48
1914	Fritz Maisel	74
1985	Rickey Henderson	80
1986	Rickey Henderson	87
1988	**Rickey Henderson**	93

Most Pinch At Bats

1903	Monte Beville	4
1904	Dave Fultz	6
1906	Joe Yeager	**18
1909	Charlie Hemphill	24
1915	Ray Caldwell	33
1952	Johnny Mize	48
1953	**Johnny Mize**	61

Most Pinch Hits

1903	Monte Beville	1
1904	Dave Fultz	2
	Deacon McGuire	2
1906	Joe Yeager	3
1909	Charlie Hemphill	6
1915	Ray Caldwell	9
1947	Bobby Brown	9
1951	Johnny Mize	9
1952	Johnny Mize	10
1953	**Johnny Mize**	19

Highest Pinch Batting Average
(Minimum 10 At Bats)

1913	Ray Caldwell	.210
1915	Ray Caldwell	.272
1916	**Les Nunamaker**	.545

Longest Hitting Streak

1907	Hal Chase	27
1919	Roger Peckinpaugh	29
1931	Earle Combs	29
1941	Joe DiMaggio	***56

RECORD HOLDERS LIST

1	Babe Ruth	23
2	Willie Keeler	16
3	Jimmy Williams	12
4	Birdie Cree	10
5	Lou Gehrig	6
5	Hal Chase	6
7	Wally Pipp	5
8	Wid Conroy	4
8	Ray Caldwell	4
8	Earle Combs	4
11	Don Mattingly	3
11	Bobby Richardson	3
11	Roger Peckinpaugh	3
11	Charlie Hemphill	3
11	Mickey Mantle	3
11	Johnny Mize	3
11	Dave Fultz	3
11	Rickey Hendersen	3
19	John Anderson	2

JOE DiMAGGIO
His 56-game hitting streak has been called baseball's greatest achievement.

19	Herm McFarland	2
19	Guy Zinn	2
19	Harry Wolter	2
19	Joe Yeager	2
19	Monte Beville	2
19	Roy White	2
19	Bob Meusel	2
27	Roger Maris	1
27	Frank Baker	1
27	Lefty Davis	1
27	Roy Hartzell	1
27	Tony Lazzeri	1
27	Bobby Bonds	1
27	Fritz Maisel	1
27	Deacon McGuire	1
27	Joe DiMaggio	1
27	Les Nunamaker	1
27	Chris Chambliss	1
27	Red Rolfe	1
27	Aaron Ward	1
27	John Ganzel	1
27	Bobby Brown	1

JOE DiMAGGIO'S 56-GAME HITTING STREAK

Hal Chase was the first Yankee to put together a hitting streak worthy of mention. In 1907 the solid-hitting first baseman was successful in 27 straight games.

In 1919 Roger Peckinpaugh, who was one of the greatest Yankee shortstops, hit safely in 29 games to set a new mark.

It took 12 years before Earle Combs would tie this record, as he hit safely in 29 games in 1931.

The greatest of all hitting streaks took place in 1941. Joltin' Joe DiMaggio went on a hitting spree from May 15th to July 16th. Every Major League player has tried to break this record for the last 46 years, and all have failed. Willie Keeler and Pete Rose came the closest, with 44 games each. (Keeler had the Major League record before Joe D's magnificent achievement.)

During the streak the "Yankee Clipper" had 223 at bats and 91 hits, including 56 singles, 16 doubles, 4 triples, and 15 home runs. He scored 56 runs and drove in 55 and had a batting average of .408. DiMaggio's slugging percentage was a whopping .717, as he accumulated 35 extra base hits for 160 total bases. (He also got a hit in the All-Star game, which means he actually hit in 57 games.)

SUMMARY AND HIGHLIGHTS

It is no surprise to see the great Babe Ruth at the top of the records list. The Babe was the first Yankee to rap more than 200 hits in one season, and three times he set home run and batting average records. The mighty "Bambino" had such a great year in 1920 that even he himself could not break his home run percentage and slugging titles. The "Sultan of Swat" belted 54 round-trippers for an amazing 11.8 percentage, and he slugged an unbelievable .847. Both marks remain unbroken Major League records.

Most sluggers have a tendency to strike out a lot, and the Babe had his share of whiffs. But a quick look at the record book shows that he led the league only one time in strikeouts. Considering that that year he batted .393, had a league-leading 41 home runs, and received a phenomenal number of bases on balls (170, which is still an unbroken Major League record), his strikeouts suddenly become insignificant.

In the early years of the Yankee franchise Birdie Cree was one of the hitting stars. He could fly like a bird, and his blazing speed enabled him to

RECORD PROFILE
BABE RUTH
SEASON BATTING RECORDS

Year	Record	Value	Note
1920	Most Home Runs	54	1 year before broken
	Highest Home Run Percentage	11.8	**NEVER BROKEN**
	Most Extra Base Hits	99	1 year before broken
	Most Total Bases	388	1 year before broken
	Highest Batting Average	.376	1 year before broken
	Highest Slugging Percentage	.847	**NEVER BROKEN**
	Most Bases on Balls	148	3 years before broken
	Most RBIs	137	1 year before broken
	Most Runs Scored	158	1 year before broken
1921	Most Hits	204	2 years before broken
	Most Doubles	44	6 years before broken
	Most Home Runs	59	6 years before broken
	Most Extra Base Hits	119	**NEVER BROKEN**
	Most Total Bases	457	**NEVER BROKEN**
	Highest Batting Average	.378	2 years before broken
	Most RBIs	170	6 years before broken
	Most Runs Scored	177	**NEVER BROKEN**
1923	Most Hits	205	4 years before broken
	Most Strikeouts	93	3 years before broken
	Most Doubles	45	3 years before broken
	Highest Batting Average	.393	**NEVER BROKEN**
	Most Bases on Balls	170	**NEVER BROKEN**
1927	Most Home Runs	60	34 years before broken

set three consecutive triples records. He was also the first Yankee to gather more than 50 extra base hits and go over the .500 slugging percentage mark.

Lou Gehrig does not have as many records as might be expected, but it must be realized that in order for him to enter the record book, he had to do better than Babe Ruth. This would be a problem that all future Yankees would have to face.

But make no mistake about it, the "Iron Horse" was one of the greatest in the game. An example of his greatness can be found in the RBI category, where he still holds the mark for most RBIs, not only as a Yankee but for the entire American League. In 1931 he broke his own record of 175 RBIs and replaced it with 184 more. And when one considers that Babe Ruth in 1927 hit 60 home runs (thus clearing the bases before Gehrig), Gehrig's 175 RBIs in that season might very well be his greatest achievement.

The slugging star prior to Babe Ruth was Wally Pipp. Compared to the mighty Babe, Pipp was a little man of 180 pounds. Pipp will always be remembered as the man who gave way to Lou Gehrig. He became the first Yankee to hit home runs in double figures (dead ball era), and his dozen homers doubled the previous record.

In modern times Bobby Richardson was the first to play in all 162 games of a 162-game schedule. Roy White accomplished the feat twice, but neither could challenge the consecutive-game streak set by Lou Gehrig, who played in every game for 13 consecutive years! His remarkable 2,130-game streak is not likely to be broken.

Of the modern-day players Don Mattingly is the glowing star. In 1986 the blossoming slugger added his name to the record book for most hits in one season. He also passed Lou Gehrig's 59-year-old doubles mark with 53 two-baggers.

One of the greatest moments in baseball history came in 1961, when Roger Maris astounded the baseball world by hitting 61 home runs, thus breaking one of the game's most cherished records. Many fans were disheartened and did not want to see this record broken. Others refused to accept it, saying Maris had the advantage of a 162-game schedule compared to Babe Ruth's 154 games.

This argument continued for seven years before a special rules committee put the matter to rest by proclaiming that baseball would have only one set of records, with no separation between the 154- and 162-game schedules. Therefore Maris's record was deemed official, and rightly so. What Roger Maris did in the 1961 season must go down as one of the greatest achievements in baseball history. When Babe Ruth hit his famous 60 home runs in 1927, he was not under the same pressure as Roger Maris, since the Babe already held the record at 59.

When it was evident that Maris had a good chance at the most prized of all records, he received hate mail and even death threats. But Maris continued playing well under horrendous conditions. He hit his 59th home run

WILLIE KEELER
One of the very first New York Yankee superstars.

RECORD PROFILE
WILLIE KEELER
SEASON BATTING RECORDS

1903	Most Games	132	1 year before broken
	Most At Bats	515	1 year before broken
	Most Hits	164	1 year before broken
	Highest Batting Average	.318	1 year before broken
	Most Runs Scored	95	3 years before broken
	Most Singles	143	1 year before broken
1904	Most Hits	186	2 years before broken
	Most Singles	162	2 years before broken
	Highest Batting Average	.343	7 years before broken
	Highest Slugging Percentage	.409	6 years before broken
1905	Most Games	149	1 year before broken
	Most At Bats	560	1 year before broken
1906	Most Games	151	8 years before broken
	Most Singles	166	**NEVER BROKEN**
	Most Runs Scored	96	14 years before broken
1904	Most Total Bases	222	2 years before broken

with plenty of time to spare, but the 60th was a long time in coming, and when he finally hit it, there were only three games left in which to break the record. He failed to pop one out in the next two games, and so it came down to the very last game of the year. Could a situation possibly be more dramatic? Roger Maris did what the oddsmakers said was virtually impossible. He hit his famous 61st home run on the last day of the season.

Sure, he had a few more at bats—50 more to be exact. But the Babe did not have to face the wicked relief pitching that Roger did. In Ruth's era there was little relief pitching, and the Babe had the advantage of hitting off tiring starting pitchers from the sixth inning on. Maris was often faced with tough, fresh lefthanded flamethrowers from the bullpen.

The pitchers were always afraid of pitching to the Babe, and they walked him more than any player in baseball history. But what Maris had to face in 1961 was even worse. Pitchers did not want to give him good pitches to hit. They did not want to go down in history as the pitcher who surrendered the 61st homer. But in spite of these tremendous difficulties Roger Maris won the battle and captured one of the most precious records the game has ever had.

While Babe Ruth lost his prized home run crown, there are seven other titles that he has not yet lost. Of his remarkable 23 season records, the Babe is still the leader in home run percentage, extra base hits, total bases, batting average, slugging percentage, runs scored, and bases on balls.

Rickey Henderson has taken over as the greatest base stealer in New York Yankee history. In his four years with the club, he has set three stolen base records, the last of which was his 93 in 1988. He is also a good bet to pass Lou Brock for the Major League career record within the next few years.

CHAPTER II

SEASON PITCHING RECORDS

PITCHING QUIZ

1. Name the Yankee pitcher who started 36 games and completed 33.
2. Do you know which Yankee pitcher made the most appearances in one season?
3. Name the only Yankee pitcher to give up more walks than Babe Ruth received when he set the record.
4. There have been four Yankee pitchers with winning percentages over .800. How many can you name?
5. This outstanding Yankee pitcher batted .364 one season. Do you know him?

DID YOU KNOW that Whitey Ford won 14 games in a row?

DID YOU KNOW that the team record for the lowest ERA by a starting pitcher is 1.64 and that it has not been broken in 45 years? Who holds this marvelous record?

DID YOU KNOW that Ron Guidry is the all-time leader in strikeouts with 248 and shutouts with nine?

Most Appearances

1903	Jack Chesbro	40
1904	Jack Chesbro	55
1947	Joe Page	56
1949	Joe Page	60
1961	Luis Arroyo	65
1965	Pedro Ramos	65
1967	Dooley Womack	65
1974	Sparky Lyle	66
1977	Sparky Lyle	72
1985	Dave Righetti	74
1986	Dave Righetti	74

Most Starts

1903	Jack Chesbro	36
1904	Jack Chesbro	*51

Most Complete Games

1903	Jack Chesbro	33
1904	Jack Chesbro	*48

Most Wins

1903	Jack Chesbro	21
1904	Jack Chesbro	*41

Most Losses

1903	Jack Chesbro	16
1904	Jake Powell	19
1907	Al Orth	21
1908	Joe Lake	21
1912	Russ Ford	21
1925	Sam Jones	21

Highest Winning Percentage

1903	Jack Chesbro	.568
1904	Jack Chesbro	.759
1910	Russ Ford	.813
1934	Lefty Gomez	.839
1961	Whitey Ford	.862
1978	Ron Guidry	.893

Lowest ERA

1903	Clark Griffith	2.70
1904	Jack Chesbro	1.82
1910	Russ Ford	1.65
1919	Carl Mays	1.65
1943	Spud Chandler	1.64

Most Innings

1903	Jack Chesbro	325
1904	Jack Chesbro	*454

Most Hits Allowed

1903	Jack Chesbro	300
1904	Jack Chesbro	337

Most Bases on Balls

1903	Jack Chesbro	74
1904	Jake Powell	92
1905	Bill Hogg	101
1910	Hippo Vaughn	107
1915	Ray Caldwell	107
1918	Slim Love	116
1936	Monte Pearson	135
1949	Tommy Byrne	179

Most Strikeouts

1903	Jack Chesbro	147
1904	Jack Chesbro	239
1978	Ron Guidry	248

Most Shutouts

1903	Jesse Tannehill	2
1904	Jack Chesbro	6
1910	Russ Ford	8
1964	Whitey Ford	8
1978	Ron Guidry	9

Longest Winning Streak .

1904	Jack Chesbro	14
1961	Whitey Ford	14

Longest Losing Streak

1908	Bill Hogg	9
1967	Thad Tillotson	9

Most Wild Pitches

1964	Al Downing	14

Most Hit Batsmen

1909	Jack Warhop	26

* American League Record
** Major League Record
*** Unbroken Major League Record

RICH "GOOSE" GOSSAGE

BOB TURLEY

RELIEF PITCHING RECORDS

Most Appearances

1903	Harry Howell	10
1905	Clark Griffith	**18
1914	King Cole	18
1917	Bob Shawkey	26
1918	George Mogridge	26
1927	Wilcy Moore	38
1929	Wilcy Moore	41
1947	Joe Page	54
1948	Joe Page	54
1949	Joe Page	*60
1961	Luis Arroyo	65
1965	Pedro Ramos	65
1967	Dooley Womack	65
1974	Sparky Lyle	66
1977	Sparky Lyle	72
1985	**Dave Righetti**	74
1986	**Dave Righetti**	74

Most Wins

1903	Clark Griffith	1
	Harry Howell	1
1904	Jack Chesbro	*3
1905	Clark Griffith	6
1916	Bob Shawkey	8
1927	Wilcy Moore	**13
1947	Joe Page	*14
1961	**Luis Arroyo**	*15

Most Losses

1903	Jack Chesbro	1
	Bill Wolfe	1
1904	Walter Clarkson	2
1905	Clark Griffith	3
1909	Jack Warhop	3
1918	George Mogridge	**7
1942	Johnny Murphy	10
1971	Lindy McDaniel	10
1978	**Goose Gossage**	11

The **Boston Record**, *upon learning that Tom Yawkey had bought Hank Johnson from the Yankees (after former owner Harry Frazee had sold 15 Red Sox players to the Yankees in five years), headlined "MAN BITES DOG."*

John Schulian on Billy Martin: "A mouse studying to be a rat."

Most Saves

1904	Clark Griffith	1
	Walter Clarkson	1
1905	Clark Griffith	3
1907	Bob Keefe	3
1908	Jack Chesbro	3
1909	Jack Warhop	4
1916	Bob Shawkey	8
1922	Sam Jones	8
1927	Wilcy Moore	13
1939	Johnny Murphy	19
1949	Joe Page	**27
1961	Luis Arroyo	**29
1970	Lindy McDaniel	29
1972	Sparky Lyle	*35
1986	**Dave Righetti**	***46

Most Wins Plus Saves

1903	None	
1904	Jack Chesbro	3
1905	Clark Griffith	7
1912	Jack Warhop	7
1916	Bob Shawkey	15
1927	Wilcy Moore	26
1947	Joe Page	**31
1949	Joe Page	**40
1961	Luis Arroyo	**44
1972	Sparky Lyle	44
1986	**Dave Righetti**	***54

Highest Winning Percentage (Minimum 15 Games)

1903	None	
1904	None	
1905	Clark Griffith (6–3)	.667
1908	Rube Manning (4–1)	.800
1926	Waite Hoyt (4–1)	.800
1927	Wilcy Moore (13–3)	.812
1938	Johnny Murphy (8–1)	.889
1954	Bob Grim (8–0)	1.000

Lowest ERA (Minimum 15 Games)

1903	None	
1904	None	
1905	Clark Griffith	1.67
1974	Sparky Lyle	1.66
1981	**Goose Gossage**	0.77

Most Innings

1929	Wilcy Moore	62
1937	Johnny Murphy	79
1938	Johnny Murphy	91
1947	Joe Page	125
1949	Joe Page	135
1973	Lindy McDaniel	141

Most Hits Allowed

1929	Wilcy Moore	64
1937	Johnny Murphy	72
1947	Joe Page	105
1948	Joe Page	116
1973	Lindy McDaniel	133

Most Bases on Balls

1929	Wilcy Moore	19
1935	Johnny Murphy	22
1936	Johnny Murphy	26
1937	Johnny Murphy	35
1940	Johnny Murphy	40
1947	Joe Page	72
1948	Joe Page	75

Most Strikeouts

1929	Wilcy Moore	21
1935	Johnny Murphy	22
1936	Johnny Murphy	26
1937	Johnny Murphy	35
1947	Joe Page	116
1978	Goose Gossage	122

PITCHERS BATTING RECORDS

Most At Bats

1903	Jack Chesbro	124
1904	Jack Chesbro	174

Most Hits

1903	Jesse Tannehill	26
1904	Jack Chesbro	41
1918	Ray Caldwell	44
1921	Carl Mays	49

Most Home Runs

1903	Jack Chesbro	2
1915	Ray Caldwell	4
1930	Red Ruffing	4
1936	Red Ruffing	5

Highest Batting Average

1903	Jesse Tannehill	.234
1904	Ambrose Puttman	.278
1905	Ambrose Puttman	.313
1921	Carl Mays	.343
1930	Red Ruffing	.364

CHRONOLOGY OF 20-GAME WINNERS

1903	Jack Chesbro	21–15†
1904	Jack Chesbro	41–12†
	Jake Powell	23–19
1906	Al Orth	27–17
	Jack Chesbro	24–16†
1910	Russ Ford	26–6
1911	Russ Ford	22–11
1916	Bob Shawkey	24–14
1919	Bob Shawkey	20–13
1920	Carl Mays	26–11‡
1922	Joe Bush	26–7‡
	Bob Shawkey	20–12
1923	Sad Sam Jones	21–8‡
1924	Herb Pennock	21–9§
1926	Herb Pennock	21–11§
1927	Waite Hoyt	22–7§
1928	Waite Hoyt	23–7§
1931	Lefty Gomez	21–9†
1932	Lefty Gomez	24–7†
1934	Lefty Gomez	26–5†
1936	Red Ruffing	20–12§
1937	Red Ruffing	20–7§
	Lefty Gomez	21–11†
1938	Red Ruffing	21–7§
1939	Red Ruffing	21–7§
1942	Ernie Bonham	21–5
1943	Spud Chandler	20–4
1946	Spud Chandler	20–8
1949	Vic Raschi	21–10
1950	Vic Raschi	21–8

† Hall of Famers.
‡ Traded to the Yankees from the Red Sox.
§ Hall of Famers traded to the Yankees from the Red Sox—the Yankee success was partially due to the financial situation the Red Sox were in, the result of owner Frazee's failures in show business and his willingness to sell his best pitchers to New York.

1951	Vic Raschi	21–9
	Ed Lopat	21–9
1952	Allie Reynolds	20–8
1954	Bob Grim	20–6
1958	Bob Turley	21–7
1961	Whitey Ford	25–4†
1962	Ralph Terry	23–12
1963	Whitey Ford	24–7†.
	Jim Bouton	21–7
1965	Mel Stottlemyre	20–9
1968	Mel Stottlemyre	21–12
1969	Mel Stottlemyre	20–14
1970	Fritz Peterson	20–11
1975	Catfish Hunter	23–14†
1978	Ron Guidry	25–3
	Ed Figueroa	20–9
1979	Tommy John	21–9
1980	Tommy John	22–9
1983	Ron Guidry	21–9
1985	Ron Guidry	22–6

A CHRONOLOGY OF YANKEE NO-HITTERS

| 1910 | Tom Hughes | (Aug. 30) |

Nine-inning 0–0 tie, gave up hit in tenth inning and lost game in 11th.

1923	Sad Sam Jones	(Sept. 4)
1938	Monte Pearson	(Aug. 27)
1951	Allie Reynolds	(July 12)
	Allie Reynolds	(Sept. 28)

Only Yankee to pitch two no-hitters in one season and in a career.

| 1956 | Don Larson | (Oct. 8) |

Perfect game in World Series. Only pitcher in baseball history to do so.

| 1983 | Dave Righetti | (July 4) |

Red Ruffing on Joe DiMaggio: "You saw him standing out there in center field, and you knew you had a pretty damn good chance of winning the game."

RECORD HOLDERS LIST

1	Jack Chesbro	25
2	Joe Page	16
3	Johnny Murphy	13
4	Clark Griffith	10
4	Wilcy Moore	10
6	Sparky Lyle	7
7	Luis Arroyo	5
8	Dave Righetti	4
8	Jack Warhop	4
8	Bob Shawkey	4
8	Russ Ford	4
8	Lindy McDaniel	4
13	Goose Gossage	3
13	Whitey Ford	3
13	Ron Guidry	3
16	Sam Jones	2
16	Bill Hogg	2
16	George Mogridge	2
16	Jake Powell	2
16	Pedro Ramos	2
16	Dooley Womack	2
16	Harry Howell	2
23	Bob Grim	1
23	Bill Wolfe	1
23	Waite Hoyt	1
23	King Cole	1
23	Al Downing	1
23	Walter Clarkson	1
23	Thad Tillotson	1
23	Ray Caldwell	1
23	Jessie Tannehill	1
23	Carl Mays	1
23	Rube Manning	1
23	Joe Lake	1
23	Spud Chandler	1
23	Bob Keefe	1
23	Lefty Gomez	1
23	Hippo Vaughn	1
23	Slim Love	1
23	Monte Pearson	1
23	Al Orth	1
23	Tommy Byrne	1

DID YOU KNOW that the most home runs ever hit by a Yankee pitcher in one season is five by Red Ruffing?

SUMMARY AND HIGHLIGHTS

Jack Chesbro was the first outstanding starting pitcher for the New York Yankees, and he was the first one to enter the Hall of Fame. This honor was well deserved, as Chesbro was one of the last "iron horse" pitchers in the American League. At 5′ 9″ and 180 pounds "Happy Jack" didn't look like a giant, but he earned his nickname by always being happy to take the mound when it was his turn.

Second on the records list is popular relief pitcher Joe Page. Although Wilcy Moore and Johnny Murphy were excellent relievers, Joe Page was the fireman who really excited Yankee fans and made the art of relief pitching as popular as we know it today.

Johnny "Grandma" Murphy was actually called the first fireman, and he is not far behind the accomplishments of Joe Page. Murphy was the star Yankee reliever in the late 1930s and put 13 records in the book.

The very first notable relief pitcher was player-manager Clark Griffith in 1903. He and Harry Howell were the first two pitchers to win games in relief, in 1903. Griffith was also the first to register a save (1904). Griffith did even better in 1905, winning six and losing three in relief with an overall ERA of 1.67.

Prior to Johnny Murphy, Wilcy Moore held down the number-one reliever job. He starred in 1927 with 13 wins and only three losses, which not only set a Yankee record but a Major League mark as well. In addition to his 13–3 record Moore also recorded 13 saves, which at that time was the greatest achievement of any relief pitcher in baseball.

The Yankees have been blessed with great relief pitchers, and one of the proofs is that as a team they have registered more saves than any other in baseball.

Whereas Clark Griffith was the first fine Yankee reliever, and Wilcy Moore, Johnny Murphy, and Joe Page followed, Sparky Lyle, Goose Gossage, and Dave Righetti are the modern greats. It would be a tough choice to have to pick only one to come out of the bullpen.

Sparky Lyle, the man with the tremendous slider, was the first Yankee to appear in 70 games and go over the 30-saves mark. In 1972, Sparky had nine wins and 35 saves in 72 games.

Goose Gossage terrorized batters for six years, averaging 25 saves per year. In 1981 he was almost unhittable as he posted a brilliant 0.77 ERA, and his 122 strikeouts in 1978 is still an unbroken mark.

When the front office converted Dave Righetti, their star starting pitcher, into a reliever, many doubts were aired. But "Rags" removed those doubts by saving 31 games in 1984, his first year in the pen. Since then he has not saved fewer than 30 games per year and even celebrated his new job by setting a new Major League record in saves with 46 (1986).

The only Yankee to have more than 30 (and 40) wins in a season is Jack Chesbro, who dominates the Yankees' starting pitchers' marks. But the Yankees did not win 33 pennants and 22 World Series without numerous other outstanding starting pitchers.

JACK CHESBRO

RECORD PROFILE
JACK CHESBRO
SEASON PITCHING RECORDS

1903	Most Appearances	40	1 year before broken
	Most Innings	325	1 year before broken
	Most Wins	21	1 year before broken
	Most Losses	16	1 year before broken
	Highest Winning Percentage	.568	1 year before broken
	Most Starts	36	1 year before broken
	Most Complete Games	33	1 year before broken
	Most Hits Allowed	300	1 year before broken
	Most Bases on Balls	74	1 year before broken
	Most Strikeouts	147	1 year before broken
	Most Relief Losses	1	2 years before broken
1904	Most Appearances	55	57 years before broken
	Most Wins	41	**NEVER BROKEN**
	Most Innings	454	**NEVER BROKEN**
	Lowest ERA	1.82	1 year before broken
	Highest Winning Percentage	.759	6 years before broken
	Most Starts	51	**NEVER BROKEN**
	Most Completions	48	**NEVER BROKEN**
	Most Strikeouts	239	74 years before broken
	Most Shutouts	6	6 years before broken
	Most Consecutive Wins	14	**NEVER BROKEN**
	Most Relief Wins	3	1 year before broken
	Most Wins Plus Saves	3	1 year before broken
	Most Hits Allowed	337	**NEVER BROKEN**
1908	Most Saves	3	1 year before broken

JOE PAGE
A premier Yankee fireman.

RECORD PROFILE
JOE PAGE
SEASON PITCHING RECORDS

1947	Most Appearances	56	2 years before broken
	Most Relief Games	54	2 years before broken
	Most Wins	14	14 years before broken
	Most Wins Plus Saves	31	2 years before broken
	Most Innings	125	2 years before broken
	Most Hits Allowed	105	1 year before broken
	Most Bases on Balls	72	1 year before broken
	Most Strikeouts	116	31 years before broken
1948	Most Relief Games	54	1 year before broken
	Most Hits Allowed	116	25 years before broken
	Most Bases on Balls	75	**NEVER BROKEN**
1949	Most Relief Games	60	12 years before broken
	Most Saves	27	12 years before broken
	Most Wins Plus Saves	40	12 years before broken
	Most Innings	135	25 years before broken
	Most Total Games	60	12 years before broken

In 1910 rookie Russ Ford became the first starting pitcher to turn in a winning percentage over .800. The spectacular rookie won 26 while losing only six and had eight shutouts and a remarkable ERA of 1.65. It was the greatest performance of any Yankee rookie pitcher in the history of the franchise. (And still is.)

Lefty Gomez was the second pitcher to sparkle with an above-.800 winning percentage, in 1934. "Goofy" was one of his nicknames, but he certainly didn't act that way on the mound when he won 26, lost five, tossed eight shutouts, and registered a magnificent winning percentage of .839 in 1934.

Gomez's record lasted more than a quarter century before another lefty, Whitey Ford, would break it. In 1961 the smooth-throwing hurler won 25 and lost only four times. It represented a sizzling winning percentage of .862. Many thought this record would never be broken, but New York fans will never forget the 1978 season Ron Guidry had. This 161-pounder (and another lefty) was called "Louisiana Lightning" due to his blazing fastball and broke Ford's record by posting an unbelievable 25–3 mark with nine shutouts and a cool 1.74 ERA. In doing so, the swift lefthander sent 248 batters grumbling back to their dugouts with bat in hand.

LEFTY GOMEZ

JIM "CATFISH" HUNTER

DAVE RIGHETTI

DON LARSEN
The only pitcher in baseball to throw a perfect game in the World Series!

CHAPTER III

SEASON FIELDING RECORDS

FIELDING QUIZ

1. The Yankee first base putouts record has not been broken in 66 years. Who holds it?
2. Name the Yankee second baseman who created five consecutive new putout records.
3. Do you know the Yankee third baseman with the highest fielding average?
4. Between Earle Combs and Joe DiMaggio, which centerfielder has the most records?
5. Only one Yankee catcher has gone through a season without making an error. Name him.

DID YOU KNOW that Babe Ruth had more chances in right field than any other rightfielder?

DID YOU KNOW that Phil Rizzuto turned more DPs than any other Yankee shortstop?

DID YOU KNOW that Graig Nettles is the only Yankee third baseman with more than 400 assists?

FIRST BASE

Most Putouts

1903	John Ganzel	1,385
1906	Hal Chase	1,504
1916	Wally Pipp	1,513
1917	Wally Pipp	1,609
1920	Wally Pipp	1,649
1922	**Wally Pipp**	1,667

Most Assists

1903	John Ganzel	94
1916	Wally Pipp	99
1917	Wally Pipp	109
1942	Buddy Hassett	118
1964	Joe Pepitone	121

Most Errors

1903	John Ganzel	18
1905	Hal Chase	31
1906	Hal Chase	33
1907	Hal Chase	34
1911	Hal Chase	36

Fewest Errors

1903	John Ganzel	18
1904	John Ganzel	16
1914	Charlie Mullen	6
1963	Joe Pepitone	6
1965	Joe Pepitone	3

Most Double Plays

1903	John Ganzel	68
1910	Hal Chase	68
1915	Wally Pipp	85
1916	Wally Pipp	89
1917	Wally Pipp	97
1920	Wally Pipp	101
1921	Wally Pipp	116
1929	Lou Gehrig	134
1938	**Lou Gehrig**	**157

* American League Record
** Major League Record
*** Unbroken Major League Record

Most Chances Per Game

1903	John Ganzel	11.6
1919	Wally Pipp	11.6
1922	Wally Pipp	11.6

Most Total Chances

1903	John Ganzel	1,497
1906	Hal Chase	1,621
1916	Wally Pipp	1,625
1917	Wally Pipp	1,735
1920	Wally Pipp	1,764
1922	**Wally Pipp**	1,768

Highest Fielding Percentage

1903	John Ganzel	.988
1904	John Ganzel	.988
1914	Charlie Mullen	.994
1924	Wally Pipp	.994
1929	Lou Gehrig	.994
1934	Lou Gehrig	.994
1936	Lou Gehrig	.994
1947	George McQuinn	.994
1963	Joe Pepitone	.995
1965	**Joe Pepitone**	.997
1978	**Chris Chambliss**	.997
1981	**Bob Watson**	.997

SECOND BASE

Most Putouts

1903	Jimmy Williams	266
1904	Jimmy Williams	315
1905	Jimmy Williams	335
1906	Jimmy Williams	336
1907	Jimmy Williams	357
1922	Aaron Ward	358
1923	Aaron Ward	387
1943	Joe Gordon	407
1944	**George Stirnweiss**	433

Most Assists

1903	Jimmy Williams	438
1904	Jimmy Williams	*465
1919	Del Pratt	491
1920	**Del Pratt**	515

Most Errors

1903	Jimmy Williams	32
1904	**Jimmy Williams**	40

Fewest Errors		
1903	Jimmy Williams	32
1905	Jimmy Williams	25
1909	Frank LaPorte	23
1910	Frank LaPorte	15
1947	George Stirnweiss	13
1953	Billy Martin	12
1967	**Horace Clarke**	8

Most Double Plays		
1903	Jimmy Williams	59
1915	Luke Boone	59
1918	Del Pratt	82
1923	Aaron Ward	86
1929	Tony Lazzeri	101
1939	Joe Gordon	116
1940	Joe Gordon	116
1942	Joe Gordon	121
1961	**Bobby Richardson**	136

Most Chances Per Game		
1903	Jimmy Williams	5.6
1904	Jimmy Williams	5.6
1906	Jimmy Williams	5.6
1907	Jimmy Williams	5.6
1913	Roy Hartzell	5.7
1914	Luke Boone	6.2
1945	**George Stirnweiss**	6.3

Most Total Chances		
1903	Jimmy Williams	736
1904	Jimmy Williams	820
1919	Del Pratt	832
1920	Del Pratt	895
1943	Joe Gordon	926
1944	**George Stirnweiss**	931

Highest Fielding Percentage		
1903	Jimmy Williams	.957
1905	Jimmy Williams	.964
1907	Jimmy Williams	.966
1917	Fritz Maisel	.967
1918	Del Pratt	.969
1919	Del Pratt	.969
1920	Del Pratt	.971
1922	Aaron Ward	.974
1923	Aaron Ward	**.980
1944	George Stirnweiss	.982
1947	George Stirnweiss	.985
1948	**George Stirnweiss**	**.993

SHORTSTOP

Most Putouts		
1903	Kid Elberfeld	221
1904	Kid Elberfeld	237
1905	Kid Elberfeld	244
1907	Kid Elberfeld	295
1914	**Roger Peckinpaugh**	356

Most Assists		
1903	Kid Elberfeld	291
1904	Kid Elberfeld	432
1908	Neal Ball	438
1914	Roger Peckinpaugh	500
1922	**Everett Scott**	538

Most Errors		
1903	Kid Elberfeld	48
1904	Kid Elberfeld	48
1905	Kid Elberfeld	57
1908	Neal Ball	80

Fewest Errors		
1903	Kid Elberfeld	48
1904	Kid Elberfeld	48
1906	Kid Elberfeld	42
1909	John Knight	38
1910	John Knight	32
1918	Roger Peckinpaugh	28
1920	Roger Peckinpaugh	28
1923	Everett Scott	27
1924	Everett Scott	27
1939	Frank Crosetti	26
1946	Phil Rizzuto	26
1947	Phil Rizzuto	25
1948	Phil Rizzuto	17
1950	Phil Rizzuto	14
1956	Gil McDougald	14
1963	Tony Kubek	13
1976	**Fred Stanley**	7

Most Double Plays		
1903	Kid Elberfeld	40
1904	Kid Elberfeld	44
1914	Roger Peckinpaugh	45
1915	Roger Peckinpaugh	60
1917	Roger Peckinpaugh	*84
1931	Lynn Lary	85
1938	Frank Crosetti	*120
1950	**Phil Rizzuto**	123

Most Chances Per Game

1903	Kid Elberfeld	6.2
1907	Kid Elberfeld	6.3

Most Total Chances

1903	Kid Elberfeld	560
1904	Kid Elberfeld	717
1907	Kid Elberfeld	747
1908	Neal Ball	786
1914	Roger Peckinpaugh	895
1938	Frank Crosetti	905

Highest Fielding Percentage

1903	Kid Elberfeld	.914
1904	Kid Elberfeld	.933
1914	Roger Peckinpaugh	.956
1918	Roger Peckinpaugh	.961
1920	Roger Peckinpaugh	.962
1922	Everett Scott	.964
1924	Everett Scott	.966
1939	Frank Crosetti	.968
1947	Phil Rizzuto	.969
1948	Phil Rizzuto	.973
1950	Phil Rizzuto	*.982
1976	Fred Stanley	.983

THIRD BASE

Most Putouts

1903	Wid Conroy	164
1908	Wid Conroy	179
1910	Jimmy Austin	206

Most Assists

1903	Wid Conroy	243
1908	Wid Conroy	249
1910	Jimmy Austin	284
1917	Frank Baker	317
1943	Billy Johnson	326
1961	Clete Boyer	353
1962	Clete Boyer	396
1973	Graig Nettles	410

DID YOU KNOW that when Frank Farrell and Bill Devery purchased the Baltimore franchise and moved it to New York in 1903, the purchase price was $18,000?

Most Errors

1903	Wid Conroy	36

Fewest Errors

1903	Wid Conroy	36
1904	Wid Conroy	22
1918	Frank Baker	13
1923	Joe Dugan	12
1932	Joe Sewell	9

Most Double Plays

1903	Wid Conroy	11
1906	Frank LaPorte	11
1908	Wid Conroy	12
1909	Jimmy Austin	19
1915	Fritz Maisel	20
1917	Frank Baker	21
1918	Frank Baker	30
1943	Billy Johnson	32
1945	Oscar Grimes	35
1952	Gil McDougald	38
1962	Clete Boyer	41
1965	Clete Boyer	46

Most Chances Per Game

1903	Wid Conroy	3.6
1907	George Moriarty	4.1

Most Total Chances

1903	Wid Conroy	443
1908	Wid Conroy	456
1910	Jimmy Austin	518
1917	Frank Baker	547
1962	Clete Boyer	605

Highest Fielding Percentage

1903	Wid Conroy	.919
1904	Wid Conroy	.944
1917	Frank Baker	.949
1918	Frank Baker	*.972
1923	Joe Dugan	.974
1932	Joe Sewell	.974
1977	Graig Nettles	.974
1978	Graig Nettles	.975

DID YOU KNOW that 12 years later Jacob Ruppert and Tillinghast L'Hommedius Huston purchased the Yankees for $460,000?

CATCHING

Most Putouts

1903	Monte Beville	296
1904	Deacon McGuire	530
1912	Ed Sweeney	548
1931	Bill Dickey	670
1933	Bill Dickey	721
1956	Yogi Berra	732
1964	**Elston Howard**	***939**

Most Assists

1903	Monte Beville	66
1904	Deacon McGuire	120
1912	Ed Sweeney	167
1913	**Ed Sweeney**	**180**

Most Errors

1903	Monte Beville	15
1904	Deacon McGuire	20
1912	**Ed Sweeney**	**34**

Fewest Errors

1903	Monte Beville	15
1905	Red Kleinow	10
1914	Ed Sweeney	10
1916	Les Nunamaker	8
1920	Muddy Ruel	6
1925	Benny Bengough	3
1931	Bill Dickey	3
1958	**Yogi Berra**	**0**

Most Double Plays

1903	Jack O'Connor	6
1904	Deacon McGuire	11
1911	Walter Blair	12
1916	Les Nunamaker	13
1918	Truck Hannah	16
1951	**Yogi Berra**	**25**

Joe McCarthy on Joe DiMaggio: "He was the best base runner I ever saw. He could have stole 50 to 60 bases a year if I let him. He wasn't the fastest man alive, he just knew how to run the bases better than anybody. I don't think in all the years he played for me that he ever got thrown out stretching."

Most Chances Per Game

1903	Jack O'Connor	5.4
1904	Deacon McGuire	6.9
1912	Ed Sweeney	6.9
1964	Elston Howard	6.9
1965	**Elston Howard**	**7.0**

Most Total Chances

1903	Monte Beville	377
1904	Deacon McGuire	670
1912	Ed Sweeney	749
1931	Bill Dickey	751
1933	Bill Dickey	809
1964	**Elston Howard**	***1,008**

Highest Fielding Percentage

1903	Monte Beville	.960
1904	Deacon McGuire	.970
1905	Red Kleinow	.978
1914	Ed Sweeney	.980
1916	Les Nunamaker	.983
1920	Muddy Ruel	.984
1925	Benny Bengough	.993
1931	Bill Dickey	**.996
1958	**Yogi Berra**	****1.000**

LEFT FIELD

Most Putouts

1903	Lefty Davis	176
1906	Frank Delahanty	180
1907	Wid Conroy	204
1909	Clyde Engle	299
1921	Babe Ruth	348
1976	**Roy White**	**380**

Most Assists

1903	Lefty Davis	7
1904	Pat Dougherty	14
1908	Jake Stahl	14
1909	Clyde Engle	17
1911	Birdie Cree	19
1933	**Ben Chapman**	**24**

Most Errors

1903	Lefty Davis	19
1905	Pat Dougherty	21

DID YOU KNOW that much of the New York Yankee success has been due to the many great trades or purchases they have made? Here are their eleven greatest:

1. Babe Ruth from the Red Sox for $125,000 in 1920.
2. Bob Shawkey from the Athletics for $85,000 in 1915.
3. Waite Hoyt (and three players) from the Red Sox for four second-string players in 1920.
4. Herb Pennock from the Red Sox for three second-string players and $50,000 in 1923.
5. Carl Mays from the Red Sox for two second-string players and $40,000 in 1919.
6. Roger Maris (and two players) from Kansas City for Hank Bauer, Don Larsen, Norm Siebern, and Marv Throneberry in 1959.
7. Sparky Lyle from the Red Sox for Danny Cater and Mario Guerrero in 1972.
8. Graig Nettles and Gerry Moses from Cleveland for John Ellis, Jerry Kenny, Charlie Spikes, and Rusty Torres in 1972.
9. Willie Randolph, Ken Brett, and Doc Ellis from Pittsburgh for Doc Medich in 1975.
10. Eddie Lopat from the Chicago White Sox for Aaron Robinson, Fred Bradley, and Bill Wight in 1948.
11. Red Ruffing from the Red Sox for Cedric Durst and $50,000 in 1930.

Fewest Errors

1903	Lefty Davis	19
1904	Pat Dougherty	12
1906	Frank Delahanty	9
1908	Jake Stahl	9
1913	Birdie Cree	3
1917	Hugh High	3
1934	Sammy Byrd	2
1943	Charlie Keller	2
1971	**Roy White**	**0**

Most Chances Per Game

1903	Lefty Davis	2.0
1906	Frank Delahanty	2.1
1907	Wid Conroy	2.2
1909	Clyde Engle	2.5
1921	Babe Ruth	2.5
1936	Joe DiMaggio	2.7

Most Total Chances

1903	Lefty Davis	202
1905	Pat Dougherty	205
1907	Wid Conroy	224
1909	Clyde Engle	334
1921	Babe Ruth	378
1976	**Roy White**	**394**

Highest Fielding Percentage

1903	Lefty Davis	.906
1904	Pat Dougherty	.925
1906	Frank Delahanty	.954
1907	Wid Conroy	.955
1910	Birdie Cree	.955
1911	Birdie Cree	.964
1913	Birdie Cree	.988
1934	Sammy Byrd	.988
1939	George Selkirk	.989
1943	Charlie Keller	*.994
1968	Roy White	*.997
1971	**Roy White**	***1.000

CENTER FIELD

Most Putouts

1903	Herm McFarland	207
1905	Dave Fultz	252
1907	Danny Hoffman	286
1916	Lee Magee	301
1922	Whitey Witt	312
1923	Whitey Witt	357
1924	Whitey Witt	362
1925	Earle Combs	401
1927	Earle Combs	411
1928	Earle Combs	424
1944	**Johnny Lindell**	**468**

Most Assists

1903	Dave Fultz	11
1905	Dave Fultz	14

1907	Danny Hoffman	20
1909	Ray Demmitt	22
1935	**Ben Chapman**	**25**

Most Errors

1903	Herm McFarland	14
1907	Danny Hoffman	15
1908	Charlie Hemphill	20
1909	**Ray Demmitt**	**•21**

Fewest Errors

1903	Herm McFarland	14
1904	Dave Fultz	5
1910	Charlie Hemphill	5
1914	Birdie Cree	5
1915	Hugh High	5
1936	Jake Powell	5
1939	Joe DiMaggio	5
1947	**Joe DiMaggio**	**1**

Most Double Plays

1903	Herm McFarland	2
	Dave Fultz	2
1904	Dave Fultz	2
1905	Dave Fultz	2
1907	Danny Hoffman	4
1909	**Ray Demmitt**	7
1928	**Earle Combs**	7
1935	**Ben Chapman**	7

Most Chances Per Game

1903	Dave Fultz	2.3
1904	Dave Fultz	2.3
1905	Dave Fultz	2.3
1907	Danny Hoffman	2.4
1911	Bert Daniels	2.4
1914	Birdie Cree	2.7
1918	Eddie Miller	2.8
1925	Earle Combs	2.8
1927	Earle Combs	2.8
1928	Earle Combs	3.0
1930	Harry Rice	3.0
1935	Ben Chapman	3.0
1937	Joe DiMaggio	3.0
1939	Joe DiMaggio	3.0
1944	**Johnny Lindell**	**3.2**
1985	**Rickey Henderson**	**3.2**

Most Total Chances

1903	Herm McFarland	230
1905	Dave Fultz	275
1907	Danny Hoffman	321

1916	Lee Magee	326
1922	Whitey Witt	329
1923	Whitey Witt	379
1924	Whitey Witt	382
1925	Earle Combs	422
1927	Earle Combs	431
1928	Earle Combs	444
1937	Joe DiMaggio	451
1944	**Johnny Lindell**	**484**

Highest Fielding Percentage

1903	Herm McFarland	.939
1904	Dave Fultz	.976
1914	Birdie Cree	.976
1915	Hugh High	.981
1939	Joe DiMaggio	.986
1944	Johnny Lindell	.986
1947	**Joe DiMaggio**	**••.997**

RIGHT FIELD

Most Putouts

1903	Willie Keeler	177
1904	Willie Keeler	186
1905	Willie Keeler	194
1906	Willie Keeler	213
1920	Babe Ruth	259
1923	**Babe Ruth**	**••378**

Most Assists

1903	Willie Keeler	10
1904	Willie Keeler	16
1905	Willie Keeler	17
1911	Harry Wolter	18
1915	Doc Cook	20
1920	Babe Ruth	21
1921	**Bob Meusel**	**28**

Most Errors

1903	Willie Keeler	13
1904	Willie Keeler	14
1912	Guy Zinn	20
1921	**Bob Meusel**	**20**

Fewest Errors

1903	Willie Keeler	13
1905	Willie Keeler	7
1906	Willie Keeler	3
1916	Frank Gilhooley	3
1942	Tommy Henrich	3
1946	**Tommy Henrich**	**2**

1951	Hank Bauer	2
1953	Hank Bauer	2
1954	Hank Bauer	2
1963	Roger Maris	2
1964	Roger Maris	1
1966	Roger Maris	1
1972	Johnny Callison	1

Most Double Plays

1903	Willie Keeler	4
1904	Willie Keeler	7
1911	Harry Wolter	8
1918	Frank Gilhooley	8
1921	Bob Meusel	8

Most Chances Per Game

1903	Willie Keeler	1.6
1905	Willie Keeler	1.6
1908	Willie Keeler	1.6
1910	Harry Wolter	1.7
1911	Harry Wolter	1.8
1912	Guy Zinn	1.8
1916	Frank Gilhooley	1.8
1920	Babe Ruth	2.2
1923	Babe Ruth	2.8

Most Total Chances

1903	Willie Keeler	200
1904	Willie Keeler	216
1905	Willie Keeler	218
1906	Willie Keeler	232
1920	Babe Ruth	299
1921	Bob Meusel	301
1923	Babe Ruth	**409

Highest Fielding Percentage

1903	Willie Keeler	.935
1904	Willie Keeler	.935
1905	Willie Keeler	.968
1906	Willie Keeler	.987
1942	Tommy Henrich	.987
1946	Tommy Henrich	.992
1953	Hank Bauer	.992
1964	Roger Maris	.996

RECORD HOLDERS LIST

1	Willie Keeler	25
2	Jimmy Williams	21
2	Kid Elberfeld	21
4	Wid Conroy	19
5	Wally Pipp	18

6	Dave Fultz	13
7	Roger Peckinpaugh	11
8	Earle Combs	10
8	John Ganzel	10
8	Babe Ruth	10
11	Birdie Cree	9
12	Phil Rizzuto	8
12	Ed Sweeney	8
12	Lefty Davis	8
12	Joe DiMaggio	8
12	Del Pratt	8
17	Frank Baker	7
17	Hal Chase	7
17	Deacon McGuire	7
17	Bill Dickey	7
17	George Stirnweiss	7
22	Whitey Witt	6
22	Danny Hoffman	6
22	Herm McFarland	6
22	Monte Beville	6
22	Bob Meusel	6
27	Yogi Berra	5
27	Clete Boyer	5
27	Everett Scott	5
27	Frank Crosetti	5
27	Joe Gordon	5
27	Aaron Ward	5
27	Lou Gehrig	5
27	Joe Pepitone	5
27	Clyde Engle	5
27	Roy White	5
37	Jimmy Austin	4
37	Elston Howard	4
37	Johnny Lindell	4
37	Frank Gilhooley	4
37	Tommy Henrich	4
37	Hank Bauer	4
37	Roger Maris	4
37	Ben Chapman	4
45	Les Nunamaker	3
45	Graig Nettles	3
45	Neal Ball	3
45	Frank LaPorte	3
45	Jake Stahl	3
45	Harry Wolter	3
45	Gil McDougald	3
45	Hugh High	3
53	Sammy Byrd	2
53	Pat Dougherty	2
53	Charlie Mullen	2

53	Billy Martin	2	73	Horace Clarke	1
53	Guy Zinn	2	73	Bert Daniels	1
53	Luke Boone	2	73	Eddie Miller	1
53	John Knight	2	73	Harry Rice	1
53	Fred Stanley	2	73	Jake Powell	1
53	Joe Dugan	2	73	Truck Hannah	1
53	Joe Sewell	2	73	Walter Blair	1
53	Charlie Keller	2	73	Oscar Grimes	1
53	Fritz Maisel	2	73	Lynn Lary	1
53	Billy Johnson	2	73	Bobby Richardson	1
53	Muddy Ruel	2	73	Tony Lazzeri	1
53	Benny Bengough	2	73	Buddy Hassett	1
53	Jack O'Connor	2	73	George McQuinn	1
53	Red Kleinow	2	73	Chris Chambliss	1
53	Ray Demmitt	2	73	Frank Delahanty	1
53	Lee Magee	2	73	Doc Cook	1
53	George Selkirk	2	73	Johnny Callison	1

SUMMARY AND HIGHLIGHTS

Due to the vast differences in playing fields and gloves, it is almost impossible to determine who the greatest fielders are.

The early players had the most errors records because the playing fields and gloves were not very good.

The dead ball, which was difficult to hit out of the infield, gave the pioneer players the advantage in infield putouts and assists. When the live ball came into play, the outfielders were able to break the putouts and assists marks of the earlier players.

However, there are some outstanding fielding achievements that indicate some players were greater than others.

In 1932 the gloves had improved greatly from the gloves of the first two decades, and Joe Sewell committed only nine errors at third base. The gloves of the 1950s through the 1980s were much better than the 1932 model Joe Sewell used, yet no Yankee third baseman has been able to go through a season with fewer than nine errors.

Catchers' mitts are the most difficult of gloves to catch with, yet Yogi Berra went through the 1958 season to become the first and only Yankee catcher to not make a single error.

In 1971 Roy White duplicated Berra's feat but had it a bit easier, as Roy accomplished his perfecto in left field.

Twenty-two outfielders in Major League history have had perfect fielding seasons. Danny Litwhiler (Philadelphia Phillies) was the first, in 1942. Curt Flood's (St. Louis Cardinals) 396 chances are the most of these players. Mickey Stanley, Ken Berry, Terry Puhl, and Brian Downing have done it twice. (Roy White had 314 chances in 1971.)

Of the pioneer players, Birdie Cree was spectacular in 1913 when he roamed the left-field pasture, only mishandling three plays. It took 21 years to break his record, and then it was only broken by one less error.

YOGI BERRA
The only Yankee catcher to go through a season without making an error.

Dave Fultz was equally effective in 1904 by making only five errors in center field. Even Joe DiMaggio committed five errors 35 years later, and it is well known that the smooth-fielding Yankee Clipper had smoother fields and much better gloves to use.

But perhaps the most outstanding fielder of those early players was Willie Keeler. Willie only booted three balls in 1906, also under bad playing conditions. Even though this was near the end of Keeler's career, Willie continued to improve his fielding and tallied 25 records, the most of any Yankee in history.

In 1914 Charlie Mullen fielded .994 at first base, as did Wally Pipp in 1924 and Lou Gehrig in 1929. Was this equivalent to Joe Pepitone's, Chris Chambliss's, and Bob Watson's .997 fielding percentage of our modern times?

DAVE WINFIELD

EVERETT SCOTT

Good health and a solid bat are also essential in creating records. It is almost impossible to create a record if a player is platooned.

Del Pratt is the only second baseman to go over the 500 mark in assists. Roger Peckinpaugh hit the 500 level right on the button, but Everett Scott is the only shortstop to go over 500 in assists.

Frank Crosetti has been the busiest shortstop in total chances and is the only one to pass the 900 level.

At third base, Graig Nettles is alone above the 400 mark in assists. He was a master at diving for balls in both directions and was one of the finest defensive third basemen in baseball. Many say Nettles was every bit as good as Brooks Robinson.

Clete Boyer was another super third baseman and is the only one to go past the 600-total-chances range.

Bill Dickey and Yogi Berra were excellent behind the plate, but Elston Howard was the most active. Ellie is the only Yankee catcher to have more than 1,000 total chances.

In center field Earle Combs was the first to record 400 putouts, and he set three marks, in 1925, 1927, and 1928.

Johnny Lindell is the leader in center field in putouts with 468 and total chances with 484.

Babe Ruth is most remembered for his sensational hitting, but he was a marvelous fielder as well. No Yankee rightfielder has caught as many fly balls or has had as many total chances as the Babe.

CHAPTER IV

ROOKIE BATTING RECORDS

BATTING QUIZ

1. The Yankee rookie at bats mark has not been broken in 52 years. Who holds this record?
2. Only two Yankee rookies have had over 200 hits. Name them.
3. Do you know the highly touted Yankee rookie who had the most strikeouts?
4. The Yankee rookie with the highest batting average and slugging percentage is not well known. Name him if you can.
5. Who is the all-time Yankee rookie home run champion?

DID YOU KNOW that Joe DiMaggio established nine rookie records in 1936 and none of them have been broken?

DID YOU KNOW that of the 20 categories of batting records, Hal Chase set new marks in 16 of them in 1905?

DID YOU KNOW that in 1925 three rookies set 11 records, but Lou Gehrig managed to set only one of them?

Most Games

1903	Monte Beville	82
1905	Hal Chase	126
1908	Neal Ball	132
1909	Jimmy Austin	136
1915	Wally Pipp	136
1925	Earle Combs	150
1926	Tony Lazzeri	155
1943	Billy Johnson	155
1962	**Tom Tresh**	**157**

Most At Bats

1903	Monte Beville	258
1905	Hal Chase	465
1909	Clyde Engle	492
1925	Earle Combs	593
1926	Mark Koenig	617
1936	**Joe DiMaggio**	**637**

Most Hits

1903	Monte Beville	50
1905	Hal Chase	116
1906	Frank LaPorte	120
1909	Clyde Engle	137
1920	Bob Meusel	151
1925	Earle Combs	203
1936	**Joe DiMaggio**	**206**

Most Singles

1903	Monte Beville	35
1905	Hal Chase	91
1908	Neal Ball	92
1909	Clyde Engle	109
1914	Doc Cook	118
1925	**Earle Combs**	**151**

Most Doubles

1903	Monte Beville	14
1905	Hal Chase	16
1906	Frank LaPorte	23
1920	Bob Meusel	40
1936	**Joe DiMaggio**	**44**

Most Triples

1903	Monte Beville	1
1904	Champ Osteen	4
	Red Kleinow	4
1905	Hal Chase	6
1906	Frank LaPorte	9
1909	Ray Demmitt	12
1915	Wally Pipp	13
1925	Earle Combs	13
1926	Tony Lazzeri	14
1936	**Joe DiMaggio**	**15**

Most Home Runs

1903	None	
1904	Champ Osteen	2
1905	Hal Chase	3
1909	Ray Demmitt	4
1912	Guy Zinn	6
1920	Bob Meusel	*11
1925	Lou Gehrig	*20
1936	**Joe DiMaggio**	**29**

Highest Home Run Percentage
(Minimum 130 At Bats)

1905	Hal Chase	0.6
1909	Ray Demmitt	0.9
1911	Otis Johnson	1.4
1912	Guy Zinn	1.5
1920	Bob Meusel	2.4
1925	Benny Paschal	**4.9
1938	**Joe Gordon**	**5.5**

Most Extra Base Hits

1903	Monte Beville	15
1905	Hal Chase	25
1906	Frank LaPorte	34
1915	Wally Pipp	37
1920	Bob Meusel	58
1936	**Joe DiMaggio**	**88**

Most Total Bases

1903	Monte Beville	66
1905	Hal Chase	153
1906	Frank LaPorte	171
1909	Clyde Engle	176
1915	Wally Pipp	176
1920	Bob Meusel	238
1925	Earle Combs	274
1936	**Joe DiMaggio**	**367**

* American League Record
** Major League Record
*** Unbroken Major League Record

Most Runs Scored

1903	Monte Beville	23
1905	Hal Chase	60
1906	Frank LaPorte	60
1909	Ray Demmitt	68
1910	Bert Daniels	68
1920	Bob Meusel	75
1925	Earle Combs	117
1936	Joe DiMaggio	*132

Most RBIs

1903	Monte Beville	29
1905	Hal Chase	49
1906	Frank LaPorte	54
1909	Clyde Engle	71
1920	Bob Meusel	83
1926	Tony Lazzeri	114
1936	Joe DiMaggio	125

Most Bases on Balls

1903	Monte Beville	16
1906	Frank LaPorte	22
1909	Ray Demmitt	55
1915	Wally Pipp	66
1962	Tom Tresh	67

Most Strikeouts

1903–12	Statistics Not Kept	
1913	Ezra Midkiff	33
1914	Doc Cook	60
1915	Wally Pipp	81
1926	Tony Lazzeri	**96
1969	Bobby Murcer	103

Highest Batting Average

1903	Monte Beville	.194
1904	Red Kleinow	.206
1905	Hal Chase	.249
1906	Frank LaPorte	.264
1909	Clyde Engle	.278
1914	Doc Cook	.283
1919	Chick Fewster	.283
1920	Bob Meusel	.328
1925	Benny Paschal	.360

DID YOU KNOW that it once took four strikes for a strikeout because the first third called strike was just a warning (1887)?

Highest Slugging Percentage

1903	Monte Beville	.256
1904	Red Kleinow	.282
1905	Hal Chase	.329
1906	Frank LaPorte	.368
1911	Otis Johnson	.378
1912	Guy Zinn	.394
1920	Bob Meusel	.517
1925	Benny Paschal	*.611

Most Pinch At Bats

1903	Monte Beville	4
1906	Frank Delahanty	5
1907	Ira Thomas	16
1923	Harvey Hendrick	24
1947	Bobby Brown	27
1954	Bob Cerv	28
1959	John Blanchard	28
1965	Ray Barker	44

Most Pinch Hits

1903	Monte Beville	1
1905	Hal Chase	1
1906	Frank Delahanty	2
1907	Ira Thomas	2
1915	Wally Pipp	2
1919	Aaron Ward	4
1920	Bob Meusel	5
1923	Harvey Hendrick	6
1947	Bobby Brown	9
1954	Bob Cerv	9
1965	Ray Barker	11

Highest Pinch Batting Average
(Minimum 10 At Bats)

1919	Aaron Ward	.285
1934	Red Rolfe	.333
1940	Buddy Rosar	.400
1962	Phil Linz	.437

DID YOU KNOW that the Cleveland Indians released Hall of Famer Joe Sewell in 1930, after he had batted .289 and struck out only three times in 353 at bats? (Sewell was signed by the Yankees in 1931 and batted .302, .272, and .273, averaging only five strikeouts for the last three years of his career.)

	RECORD HOLDERS LIST				
1	Monte Beville	16	16	Otis Johnson	2
1	Hal Chase	16	16	Bert Daniels	2
3	Bob Meusel	11	16	Frank Delahanty	2
4	Frank LaPorte	10	16	Ira Thomas	2
5	Joe DiMaggio	9	16	Harvey Hendrick	2
6	Wally Pipp	7	16	Bobby Brown	2
7	Earle Combs	6	16	Bob Cerv	2
7	Clyde Engle	6	26	Lou Gehrig	1
9	Ray Demmitt	5	26	Jimmy Austin	1
10	Tony Lazzeri	4	26	Billy Johnson	1
10	Red Kleinow	4	26	Mark Koenig	1
12	Neal Ball	3	26	Joe Gordon	1
12	Doc Cook	3	26	Ezra Midkiff	1
12	Guy Zinn	3	26	Bobby Murcer	1
12	Benny Paschal	3	26	Chick Fewster	1
16	Tom Tresh	2	26	John Blanchard	1
16	Champ Osteen	2	26	Red Rolfe	1
16	Ray Barker	2	26	Buddy Rosar	1
			26	Phil Linz	1

SUMMARY AND HIGHLIGHTS

The Yankees have had many fine rookies, but none better than the mighty Yankee Clipper, Joe DiMaggio.

Joltin' Joe was simply magnificent. So great was this soon-to-be superstar that the nine records he set in 1936 still remain unbroken after 52 long years!

The first outstanding Yankee rookie was Hal Chase in 1905. Of the 20 categories of batting records, Chase put his name in the record book 16 times. He was the first rookie to bang out more than 100 hits.

The Yankees had three outstanding rookies in 1925—Earle Combs, Lou Gehrig, and Benny Paschal.

Combs was the first of only two Yankee rookies to collect more than 200 base hits. He was also the first to score more than 100 runs—he had 117 in all.

Gehrig was the most powerful slugging rookie the team had ever had. His 20 home runs was almost double that of Bob Meusel, the previous record holder.

Benny Paschal also contributed significantly in 1925, although his career only lasted eight years as a part-time player.

In 1926 "Poosh'em Up" Tony Lazzeri arrived and promptly became the best second baseman in New York Yankee history. He set a new mark in triples and was the first to drive in more than 100 runs.

After Hal Chase set most of the original records in 1905, he had seven good seasons with the Yankees, two seasons batting over .300. In 1906 he did not let the sophomore jinx affect him as he batted a solid .323, and he batted .315 in 1911. In 1913 he was traded to the White Sox for Rollie

RECORD PROFILE
JOE DiMAGGIO
ROOKIE BATTING RECORDS
1936

Most At Bats	637	NEVER BROKEN
Most Hits	206	NEVER BROKEN
Most Doubles	44	NEVER BROKEN
Most Triples	15	NEVER BROKEN
Most Home Runs	29	NEVER BROKEN
Most Extra Base Hits	88	NEVER BROKEN
Most Total Bases	367	NEVER BROKEN
Most Runs Scored	132	NEVER BROKEN
Most RBIs	125	NEVER BROKEN

This represents one of the greatest batting feats by any rookie in Major League history.

Zeider and Babe Borton. Chase spent a season and a half with the White Sox and then went to the newly formed Federal League for the next year and a half. Cincinnati picked him up in 1916, and Chase led the league in batting with a smart .339. The smooth-fielding first baseman batted .277 and .301 in the following years before being traded to the New York Giants, where he ended his career with a lifetime batting average of .291. He was a very good player, whom the Yankees gave away. On the other hand, Babe Borton was a bust. After batting .371 for the White Sox in 1912 (39 hits in 105 at bats) he showed a lot of potential but never fulfilled it, as he batted only .130 with the Yankees in 33 games. Dizzy Dean put it best when he said, "There's no need getting excited over potential. All that is is something that has never been done yet." Dean also had another great line when he said, "It ain't braggin' if you can do it." But Babe Borton could not do it, and he was shipped off to the Federal League after his 33rd game. Rollie Zeider did not do much better, as he hit only .233 in 49 games, and he too went to the Federal League.

Wally Pipp was the next Yankee rookie of note. The soon-to-be-famous first baseman set new marks in extra base hits and total bases but batted only .246. However, Pipp improved steadily, and he soon became the greatest Yankee first baseman to that date. He had three seasons batting over .300 and three more seasons in the .290s. He did very well until that famous day when he developed a headache and asked manager Miller Huggins to replace him. Little did he know that he would never play another game for the Yankees. In 1926 he was traded to Cincinnati, where he batted .291, .260, and .283 before his retirement. The Yankees received $7,500 for him in 1926.

Earle Combs and Lou Gehrig played their entire careers with the Yankees, and both of them made it to the Hall of Fame. Combs will always be rated as one of the top three Yankee centerfielders, and being in the company of Joe DiMaggio and Mickey Mantle is quite an honor. But make no mistake about it—Earle Combs was a fabulous player, and he had an identical lifetime batting average to Joe DiMaggio's, .325. In 12 years Combs had 1,866 hits; Joe DiMaggio had 2,214 hits, and Mickey Mantle had 2,415 hits in 18 seasons.

The accomplishments of Lou Gehrig are well known. To date he has been the greatest of all Yankee first basemen. Present-day star Don Mattingly seems to have the potential to challenge Lou Gehrig for this honor, but it will take many more years of outstanding play from Mattingly before he can be called the greatest Yankee first bagger.

Tony Lazzeri appeared in 1926 and quickly became a member of Murderers' Row. The powerful-hitting second baseman stroked 162 hits, and his 114 RBIs marked the first time a Yankee rookie had gone over the magic 100 mark. "Tough Tony" enjoyed 11 more years with the Bronx Bombers, batting over .300 five times (four in a row). He was dealt to the Cubs in 1938 and batted .267. He played 14 games for the Dodgers and 13 games

RECORD PROFILE
BOB MEUSEL
ROOKIE BATTING RECORDS
1920

Most Hits	151	5 years before broken
Most Doubles	44	16 years before broken
Most Home Runs	11	5 years before broken
Highest Home Run Percentage	2.4	16 years before broken
Most Extra Base Hits	58	5 years before broken
Most Total Bases	238	6 years before broken
Most Runs Scored	75	5 years before broken
Most RBIs	83	5 years before broken
Highest Batting Average	.328	3 years before broken
Highest Slugging Percentage	.517	5 years before broken
Most Pinch Hits	5	3 years before broken

for the Giants in 1939 before looking for new employment. Lazzeri was probably the greatest second baseman in New York Yankee history. His lifetime batting average was .292.

It wouldn't be fair to discuss Yankee rookies without bringing in the name of Bob Meusel. He was the first rookie .300 hitter and the first to hit home runs in double figures. "Long Bob" was a very strong 6′ 3″ 190-pounder who possessed a magnificent arm. But his batting prowess was even better. In his brilliant ten-year career as a member of the famous Murderer's Row, Meusel batted over .300 seven times, doing it five times in a row and seven out of his first eight years.

Meusel was traded to Cincinnati for the waiver price in 1930. He batted a fine .289 for the Reds before ending his outstanding career. His lifetime batting average of .309 would indicate that he should be considered by the Hall of Fame, which thus far has not yet seen his value.

BOB MEUSEL

CHAPTER V

ROOKIE PITCHING RECORDS

PITCHING QUIZ

1. The greatest rookie pitcher joined the Yankees in 1910. Can you name him?
2. Can you name the Yankee rookie pitcher who has appeared in the most games?
3. The most strikeouts by a Yankee rookie pitcher is 209. Do you know him?
4. Who is the Yankee rookie pitcher who was also an outstanding hitter and batted .326?
5. What is the record for most wins as a Yankee rookie reliever?

DID YOU KNOW that Whitey Ford had a .900 winning percentage in his rookie year?

DID YOU KNOW that 13 rookie pitchers have hit one home run in a season but that none have ever hit two?

DID YOU KNOW that Ray Caldwell had the most hits and at bats of any Yankee rookie pitcher?

Most Appearances

1903	Bill Wolfe	20
1905	Bill Hogg	39
1908	Rube Manning	*41
1911	Ray Caldwell	41
1927	Wilcy Moore	50
1985	Brian Fisher	55

Most Starts

1903	Bill Wolfe	16
1905	Bill Hogg	22
1907	Joe Doyle	23
1908	Rube Manning	27
1910	Russ Ford	33

Most Complete Games

1903	Bill Wolfe	12
1907	Joe Doyle	15
1908	Rube Manning	19
	Joe Lake	19
1909	Jack Warhop	21
1910	Russ Ford	29

Most Wins

1903	Bill Wolfe	6
1905	Bill Hogg	9
1907	Joe Doyle	11
1908	Rube Manning	13
1910	Russ Ford	*26

Most Losses

1903	Bill Wolfe	9
1905	Bill Hogg	12
1908	Joe Lake	21

Highest Winning Percentage
(Minimum 10 Decisions)

1903	Bill Wolfe (6–9)	.400
1905	Bill Hogg (9–13)	.429
1907	Joe Doyle (11–11)	.500
1909	Jack Quinn (9–5)	.643
1910	Russ Ford (26–6)	*.813
1939	Atley Donald (13–3)	.813
1950	Whitey Ford (9–1)	.900

* American League Record
** Major League Record
*** Unbroken Major League Record

Lowest ERA

1903	Bill Wolfe	2.97
1907	Joe Doyle	2.65
1909	Jack Quinn	1.97
1910	Russ Ford	1.65

Most Innings

1903	Bill Wolfe	148
1905	Bill Hogg	205
1908	Joe Lake	269
1910	Russ Ford	300

Most Hits Allowed

1903	Bill Wolfe	143
1905	Bill Hogg	178
1908	Joe Lake	252

Most Bases on Balls

1903	Bill Wolfe	26
1905	Bill Hogg	101
1928	Hank Johnson	104
1954	Bob Grim	108

Most Strikeouts

1903	Bill Wolfe	48
1905	Bill Hogg	125
1910	Russ Ford	*209

Most Shutouts

1903	Bill Wolfe	1
1904	Ambrose Puttman	1
1905	Bill Hogg	2
1908	Joe Lake	2
	Rube Manning	2
1909	Lew Brockett	3
1910	Russ Ford	*8

Guy Bush after giving up Babe Ruth's last home run, while playing with the Boston Braves: "I never saw a ball hit so hard. It was the first ball to clear the roof at Forbes Field. He was old and fat, but he still had that great swing." (The Babe hit three home runs in his very last game.)

RELIEF PITCHING RECORDS

Most Appearances

1903	Bill Wolfe	4
1904	Walter Clarkson	9
1905	Bill Hogg	*17
1916	Slim Love	19
1925	Hank Johnson	20
1926	Myles Thomas	20
1927	Wilcy Moore	38
1958	Ryne Duren	43
1963	Hal Reniff	48
1964	Pete Mikkelsen	50
1985	Brian Fisher	55

Most Wins

1903	None	
1904	Walter Clarkson	1
1905	Bill Hogg	*4
1908	Rube Manning	4
1909	Jack Warhop	4
1910	Hippo Vaughn	4
1911	Ray Caldwell	4
1920	Rip Collins	4
1927	Wilcy Moore	**13
1979	Ron Davis	14

Most Losses

1903	Bill Wolfe	1
1905	Bill Hogg	*3
1909	Jack Warhop	3
1927	Wilcy Moore	3
1955	Johnny Kucks	3
1956	Rip Coleman	3
1958	Ryne Duren	4
1964	Pete Mikkelsen	4
1967	Thad Tillotson	6

Most Saves

1903	None	
1904	Walter Clarkson	1
1905	Bill Hogg	*1
1907	Bob Keefe	3
1916	Allan Russell	6
1927	Wilcy Moore	13
1958	Ryne Duren	*20

DID YOU KNOW that the Yankees were the first team to permanently wear numbers on their uniforms, in 1929?

Most Wins Plus Saves

1903	None	
1904	Walter Clarkson	2
1905	Bill Hogg	5
1907	Bob Keefe	6
1909	Jack Warhop	6
1916	Allan Russell	7
1927	Wilcy Moore	**26
1958	Ryne Duren	*26

*Highest Winning Percentage
(Minimum 5 Decisions)*

1905	Bill Hogg (4–3)	.571
1908	Rube Manning (4–1)	.800
1909	Jack Quinn (4–0)	1.000
1910	Hippo Vaughn (4–0)	1.000
1920	Rip Collins (4–0)	1.000
1954	Bob Grim (8–0)	1.000

Most Strikeouts

1927	Wilcy Moore	21
1955	Tom Sturdivant	48
1958	Ryne Duren	87

Lowest ERA (Minimum 30 Games)

1927	Wilcy Moore	2.28
1958	Ryne Duren	2.02

Most Innings

1927	Wilcy Moore	62
1955	Tom Sturdivant	63
1958	Ryne Duren	75
1963	Hal Reniff	89
1985	Brian Fisher	98

Most Hits Allowed

1927	Wilcy Moore	64
1964	Pete Mikkelsen	79
1979	Ron Davis	84

DID YOU KNOW that Ron Blomberg was the first designated hitter to come to bat in the Major Leagues, in 1973? He drew a base on balls.

DID YOU KNOW that Sparky Lyle appeared in 899 games, the fourth most for a pitcher in baseball history, and yet he never started a single game?

Most Bases on Balls

1927	Wilcy Moore	19
1955	Tom Sturdivant	42
1958	Ryne Duren	43

Highest Batting Average

1903	Bill Wolfe	.075
1907	Joe Doyle	.138
1908	Joe Lake	.188
1909	Lew Brockett	.283
1912	George McConnell	.297
1948	Tommy Byrne	.326

ROOKIE PITCHERS BATTING RECORDS

Most At Bats

1903	Bill Wolfe	53
1905	Bill Hogg	67
1908	Joe Lake	112
1911	Ray Caldwell	147

Most Hits

1903	Bill Wolfe	4
1904	Ambrose Puttman	5
1907	Joe Doyle	8
1908	Joe Lake	21
1911	Ray Caldwell	40

Most Home Runs

1908	Joe Lake	1
1909	Tom Hughes	1
1927	Wilcy Moore	1
	George Pipgras	1
1928	Hank Johnson	1
	Al Shealy	1
1932	Johnny Allen	1
1935	Vito Tamulis	1
1938	Steve Sundra	1
1945	Bill Bevens	1
1948	Tommy Byrne	1
1951	Tom Morgan	1
1954	Bob Grim	1

RECORD HOLDERS LIST

1	Bill Hogg	16
2	Bill Wolfe	14
3	Wilcy Moore	11
4	Russ Ford	8
5	Rube Manning	7
5	Ryne Duren	7
7	Joe Doyle	5
7	Joe Lake	5
9	Jack Warhop	4
9	Walter Clarkson	4
11	Bob Grim	3
11	Jack Quinn	3
11	Tom Sturdivant	3
14	Ray Caldwell	2
14	Pete Mikkelsen	2
14	Bob Keefe	2
14	Hank Johnson	2
14	Rip Collins	2
14	Ron Davis	2
14	Brian Fisher	2
21	Ambrose Puttman	1
21	Lew Brockett	1
21	Whitey Ford	1
21	Thad Tillotson	1
21	Rip Coleman	1
21	Johnny Kucks	1
21	Atley Donald	1

DID YOU KNOW that Yankee shortstop Everett Scott held the record for most consecutive games played—1,307—before Lou Gehrig began his streak?

DID YOU KNOW that in 1939, when Babe Dahlgren replaced Lou Gehrig at first base, he led the Yankee attack with a home run and double?

DID YOU KNOW that Joe DiMaggio belted three hits and scored three runs in his very first game with the Yankees, in 1935?

DID YOU KNOW that in 1955 Mickey Mantle hit three consecutive home runs into the center field bleachers, over the 463-feet sign?

SUMMARY AND HIGHLIGHTS

Bill Wolfe was the first Yankee rookie pitcher, in 1903. He had a losing season, with six wins and nine losses. However, he did have a good ERA of 2.97.

In being the first kid on the block, Wolfe is responsible for setting up 14 of the original records for the newcomers to improve upon.

Bill Hogg became the second rookie pitcher, in 1905, and he rewrote 14 of Wolfe's marks plus added two more of his own. Hogg also had a losing season, going 9–12, but he did improve the winning percentage and he became the first to strike out more than 100 batters.

In 1907 Slow Joe Doyle added five new records and they were all improvements. He won 11 and lost 11 to become the first .500 pitcher, lowered the ERA mark to 2.65, and completed 15 games.

Rube Manning became the most active rookie in 1908 when he appeared in 41 games and won 13 while dropping 16.

Also in 1908, Joe Lake worked in 38 games but set a new record for most innings. Lake is also tagged with having the most losses of any rookie pitcher, as he dropped 21 while winning only nine.

The first great rookie performance was turned in by Russ Ford in 1910. Ford was a sensation, winning 26 and losing only six times. In addition, he put new marks in the book for starts, complete games, winning percentage, innings, strikeouts, and shutouts. He became the first rookie to pitch 300 innings and strike out more than 200 batters. Of his eight marvelous records, seven remain unbroken.

With a year such as Ford had, it was very difficult for other rookies to enter the book until 1927, when Wilcy Moore excited Yankee fans by becoming the club's first ace relief pitcher.

In all Moore won 19 and lost seven but he was 13–3 working from the bullpen. Moore pitched in a total of 50 games, 12 as a starter and 38 in relief. His total of 50 games stood for 58 years before it was broken.

Wilcy Moore established 12 outstanding records and goes down in history as one of the greatest rookie relief pitchers in Yankee history.

It would take 52 years before another rookie reliever would win more games than Wilcy Moore. In 1979 Ron Davis was phenomenal in winning 14 while losing only two.

Rookie relief pitchers could not improve upon Moore's 1927 achievements until 1958, when Ryne Duren appeared in 43 games. Duren saved a record 20 games, and to this date no rookie has ever done better.

Duren's 20 saves, combined with his six wins, ties Moore for the 26 wins plus saves mark. Duren can also be proud of striking out the most batters and setting a sizzling 2.02 ERA, both of which remain unbroken records.

Bob Grim enters the record book as the relief pitcher with the most wins and no losses. Grim was basically a starting pitcher and had 20 starts but also worked 17 games in relief. Grim was 8–0 in relief and 12–6 as a starter for a fine 20–6 contribution in total.

RUSS FORD
Of his eight records, seven remain unbroken after 77 years.

RECORD PROFILE
RUSS FORD
1910
ROOKIE PITCHING RECORDS

Most Starts	33	NEVER BROKEN
Most Complete Games	29	NEVER BROKEN
Most Wins	26	NEVER BROKEN
Highest Winning Percentage	.813	40 years before broken
Lowest ERA	1.65	NEVER BROKEN
Most Innings	300	NEVER BROKEN
Most Strikeouts	209	NEVER BROKEN
Most Shutouts	8	NEVER BROKEN

This represents the most outstanding rookie season by any Yankee starting pitcher.

Whitey Ford is the winning percentage king with a 9–1 mark.

After Bill Wolfe established 14 of the original rookie records, he was traded to Washington after losing his first three games for the Yankees in 1904. He was 6–9 for the Senators that year, 8–14 for them in 1905, and 0–3 in 1906 before his career ended. Long Tom Hughes was also sent to Washington in that trade, and in return the Yankees received Al Orth. Hughes spent nine years with the Senators and ended his career with a 131–174 losing record. Orth put in his last six years of activity with the Yankees (1904–09) and did very well for three of those years. He went 11–6 and 18–16 and was 27–17 in 1906. when he led the league in wins, complete games, and innings pitched. He faltered from that point on, but the Yankees benefited from this trade.

Bill Hogg is at the top of the records list with 16 marks, but his records are mostly due to the fact that he was near the beginning of record keeping; his accomplishments lack quality. After going 9–13 in his rookie season, Hogg rebounded by winning 14 while losing 13 the following year. He also had a respectable year in 1907, when he won ten and lost eight, but after a 4–16 season in 1908, the Yankees released him.

Joe Doyle was the next rookie pitcher on the scene, in 1907. He was not a very active hurler for the 5 years he wore the Yankee uniform, appearing in 70 games, winning 22, and losing 22. He went to Cincinnati for an undisclosed amount of cash in 1910, but after five games with no decisions with the Reds he was gone from baseball.

Rube Manning made his debut in 1908 and created seven records. But he was a losing pitcher in all four years with the Yankees and was released in 1910.

In 1910 Russ Ford became the first truly great Yankee rookie pitcher. His fabulous 26–6 record had the Yankee fans buzzing, and they were expecting him to become a phenom. Ford did well the following year, winning 22 while dropping 11, but his fortunes did a complete turnaround, and in 1912 Ford's 21 losses were the most in Yankee history. He managed to win 13 games that year, but after another losing season in 1913 (12–18) he was released. Ford hooked up with Buffalo of the Federal League and had a spectacular season, winning 20 while losing only six. But he decided to give it up after the 1915 season, when he could win only five games while losing nine.

Ray Caldwell became a Yankee rookie in 1911 and won 14 and lost 14. After nine seasons Caldwell had a record of 95–99 and was traded to the Red Sox along with Frank Gilhooley, Slim Love, and Roxy Walters in exchange for Duffy Lewis, Ernie Shore, and Dutch Leonard (and $15,000). Caldwell was 7–4 with the Red Sox before they shipped him to Cleveland, where he finished the season with a 5–1 mark. Caldwell then had a fine year for the Indians, winning 20 and losing 10. He retired the following year (1921) with a 6–6 mark. Gilhooley, Love, and Walters were third-line players and not much help to the Red Sox. Of the players the Yankees

WILCY MOORE
The first rookie relief pitching sensation in Yankee history.

RECORD PROFILE
WILCY MOORE
1927
RELIEF PITCHING RECORDS

Most Appearances	50	58 years before broken
Most Relief Appearances	38	31 years before broken
Most Relief Wins	13	52 years before broken
Most Saves	13	31 years before broken
Most Wins Plus Saves	26	**NEVER BROKEN**
Highest Winning Percentage	.812	27 years before broken
Lowest ERA	2.28	31 years before broken
Most Innings	62	28 years before broken
Most Hits Allowed	64	37 years before broken
Most Bases on Balls	19	28 years before broken
Most Strikeouts	21	28 years before broken
Most Losses	3	31 years before broken

received in that trade, Duffy Lewis had two fair seasons, batting .272 and .271, Leonard was sent to Detroit for an undisclosed amount of cash, and Shore was 7–10 in brief opportunities with the Yankees during his last two seasons of play. In this deal, the club would have been better off keeping Caldwell, who was also an outstanding hitter.

The Yankees were hard-pressed for good rookie pitchers until Wilcy Moore came along in 1927. But after Moore's sensational 19–7 rookie season he flopped to 4–4 and 6–4 the following 2 years before being traded to the Red Sox. After a losing season with the Red Sox he was back with the Yankees, where he went 5–6 and then retired. The Yankees received Gordon Rhodes, who was 7–9 in a brief 3-year stay.

The Yankees did not do well in their rookie trades but built part of their dynasty by doing very well in their trades for starting pitchers and everyday players.

The Yankees won their first pennant in 1921 after obtaining Babe Ruth from the Red Sox for $125,000 in 1920. This was a result of the involvement of Boston's owner, Harry Frazee, in producing Broadway plays, most of which bombed. After each failure Frazee was in dire need of cash. Frazee had sent Carl Mays to the Yankees the year before, and over the next few years sent his best pitchers—Waite Hoyt, Herb Pennock, Joe Bush, and Sad Sam Jones—to the Yankees. These pitchers contributed greatly to the Yankee success during the Babe Ruth era. In addition to Ruth, the Yankees received from Boston outstanding players such as Wally Schang, Everett Scott (the best shortstop at that time), and Jumpin' Joe Dugan, who had many fine years for New York. As a result of these trades the Red Sox spent eight of the next nine years in last place while the Yankees won six pennants. ("Yankee dynasty my ear," muttered a Red Sox fan. "That was a Red Sox dynasty in Yankee uniforms.")

CHAPTER VI

ROOKIE FIELDING RECORDS

FIELDING QUIZ
---

1. Name the Yankee rookie first baseman who still has four unbroken records.
2. A famous Yankee rookie second baseman had the fewest errors and the highest fielding percentage. Name him.
3. Can you name the great Yankee centerfielder who began his career in left field and set six rookie records that still stand?
4. This slick-fielding Yankee catcher made only three errors in 1925, and this rookie mark still stands. Name him.
5. Can you name the Yankee rookie shortstop who participated in the most double plays?

DID YOU KNOW that Earle Combs was the greatest rookie centerfielder in Yankee history? He established five records that have stood since 1925.

DID YOU KNOW that in 1925 the Yankees had four rookies at four positions? Although the club finished in next-to-last place that year, these rookies later helped the team win three consecutive pennants and two World Series. The only one not to set a rookie fielding record was Lou Gehrig.

DID YOU KNOW that a future leftfielder broke two of the three Yankee rookie shortstop records set by Phil Rizzuto? His name was Tom Tresh.

FIRST BASE

Most Putouts
1903–04   No Rookies
1905   Hal Chase   1,171
1915   Wally Pipp   1,396

Most Assists
1905   Hal Chase   61
1915   Wally Pipp   85
1941   Johnny Sturm   85

Most Errors
1905   Hal Chase   *31

Fewest Errors
1905   Hal Chase   31
1915   Wally Pipp   12
1941   Johnny Sturm   12

Most Double Plays
1905   Hal Chase   *63
1915   Wally Pipp   *85
1941   Johnny Sturm   117

Most Chances Per Game
1905   Hal Chase   10.4
1915   Wally Pipp   11.1

Most Total Chances
1905   Hal Chase   1,263
1915   Wally Pipp   1,493

Highest Fielding Percentage
1905   Hal Chase   .975
1915   Wally Pipp   **.992

SECOND BASE

Most Putouts
1903–11   No Rookies
1912   Hack Simmons   162
1914   Luke Boone   238
1926   Tony Lazzeri   298
1949   Jerry Coleman   298
1976   Willie Randolph   307

* American League Record
** Major League Record
*** Unbroken Major League Record

Most Assists
1912   Hack Simmons   207
1914   Luke Boone   294
1916   Joe Gedeon   341
1926   Tony Lazzeri   *461

Most Errors
1912   Hack Simmons   21
1914   Luke Boone   22
1916   Joe Gedeon   27
1926   Tony Lazzeri   31
1938   Joe Gordon   31

Fewest Errors
1912   Hack Simmons   21
1949   Jerry Coleman   12
1952   Billy Martin   9

Most Double Plays
1912   Hack Simmons   23
1914   Luke Boone   32
1916   Joe Gedeon   55
1926   Tony Lazzeri   *72
1938   Joe Gordon   98
1949   Jerry Coleman   102

Most Chances Per Game
1912   Hack Simmons   4.4
1914   Luke Boone   6.2

Most Total Chances
1912   Hack Simmons   390
1914   Luke Boone   554
1916   Joe Gedeon   603
1926   Tony Lazzeri   790

Highest Fielding Percentage
1912   Hack Simmons   .946
1914   Luke Boone   .960
1926   Tony Lazzeri   .961
1949   Jerry Coleman   .981
1952   Billy Martin   .984

SHORTSTOP

Most Putouts
1903–07   No Rookies
1908   Neal Ball   268
1926   Mark Koenig   281

Most Assists

1908	Neal Ball	438

Most Errors

1908	Neal Ball	80

Fewest Errors

1908	Neal Ball	*80
1912	Jack Martin	36
1925	Pee Wee Wanninger	30
1941	Phil Rizzuto	29
1962	Tom Tresh	16

Most Double Plays

1908	Neal Ball	28
1925	Pee Wee Wanninger	59
1926	Mark Koenig	66
1941	Phil Rizzuto	**109

Most Chances Per Game

1908	Neal Ball	6.0

Most Total Chances

1908	Neal Ball	786

Highest Fielding Percentage

1908	Neal Ball	.898
1912	Jack Martin	.900
1925	Pee Wee Wanninger	.944
1941	Phil Rizzuto	.957
1962	Tom Tresh	.970

THIRD BASE

Most Putouts

1903–05	No Rookies	
1906	Frank LaPorte	118
1909	Jimmy Austin	176
1943	Billy Johnson	183

Most Assists

1906	Frank LaPorte	210
1909	Jimmy Austin	236
1943	Billy Johnson	326

Most Errors

1906	Frank LaPorte	35

Fewest Errors

1906	Frank LaPorte	35
1909	Jimmy Austin	32
1943	Billy Johnson	18

Most Double Plays

1906	Frank LaPorte	11
1909	Jimmy Austin	*19
1943	Billy Johnson	*32

Most Chances Per Game

1906	Frank LaPorte	3.2
1909	Jimmy Austin	4.0

Most Total Chances

1906	Frank LaPorte	363
1909	Jimmy Austin	444
1943	Billy Johnson	527

Highest Fielding Percentage

1906	Frank LaPorte	.904
1909	Jimmy Austin	**.928
1943	Billy Johnson	**.966

CATCHING

Most Putouts

1903	Monte Beville	296
1916	Roxy Walters	346
1929	Bill Dickey	476
1970	Thurmon Munson	631

Most Assists

1903	Monte Beville	66
1904	Red Kleinow	66
1907	Ira Thomas	90
1916	Roxy Walters	102
1918	Truck Hannah	111

Most Errors

1903	Monte Beville	15
1907	Ira Thomas	17
1909	Ed Sweeney	20

Fewest Errors

1903	Monte Beville	15
1916	Roxy Walters	12
1918	Truck Hannah	12
1919	Muddy Ruel	11
1925	Benny Bengough	3

Most Double Plays

1903	Monte Beville	4
1904	Red Kleinow	5
1907	Ira Thomas	7
1909	Ed Sweeney	7
1916	Roxy Walters	13
1918	**Truck Hannah**	16

Most Chances Per Game

1903	Monte Beville	5.0
1904	Red Kleinow	5.7
1909	Ed Sweeney	6.1
1916	**Roxy Walters**	7.1

Most Total Chances

1903	Monte Beville	377
1909	Ed Sweeney	377
1916	Roxy Walters	460
1918	Truck Hannah	466
1929	Bill Dickey	583
1970	**Thurman Munson**	719

Highest Fielding Percentage

1903	Monte Beville	.960
1904	Red Kleinow	.966
1918	Truck Hannah	.974
1919	Muddy Ruel	.975
1925	**Benny Bengough**	**.993

LEFT FIELD

Most Putouts

1903–05	No Rookies	
1906	Frank Delahanty	180
1909	Clyde Engle	*299
1936	Joe DiMaggio	339

Most Assists

1906	Frank Delahanty	7
1909	Clyde Engle	*17
1936	Joe DiMaggio	22

Most Errors

1906	Frank Delahanty	9
1909	Clyde Engle	18

Fewest Errors

1906	Frank Delahanty	9
1936	Joe DiMaggio	8

Most Double Plays

1906	Frank Delahanty	1
1909	Clyde Engle	*5

Most Chances Per Game

1906	Frank Delahanty	2.1
1909	Clyde Engle	2.5
1936	Joe DiMaggio	2.7

Most Total Chances

1906	Frank Delahanty	196
1909	Clyde Engle	*334
1936	Joe DiMaggio	369

Highest Fielding Percentage

1906	Frank Delahanty	.954
1936	Joe DiMaggio	*.978

CENTER FIELD

Most Putouts

1903–08	No Rookies	
1909	Ray Demmitt	185
1925	Earle Combs	*401

Most Assists

1909	Ray Demmitt	22

Most Errors

1909	Ray Demmitt	*21

Fewest Errors

1909	Ray Demmitt	21
1925	Earle Combs	9
1980	Bobby Brown	9

Most Double Plays

1909	Ray Demmitt	7

Most Chances Per Game

1909	Ray Demmitt	2.1
1925	Earle Combs	2.8

Most Total Chances

1909	Ray Demmitt	228
1925	Earle Combs	*422

Highest Fielding Percentage

1909	Ray Demmitt	.908
1925	Earle Combs	*.979

RIGHT FIELD

Most Putouts

1903–11	No Rookies	
1912	Guy Zinn	158
1914	Doc Cook	171
1939	**Charlie Keller**	**213**

Most Assists

1912	Guy Zinn	9
1914	**Doc Cook**	**15**

Most Errors

1912	Guy Zinn	20

Fewest Errors

1912	Guy Zinn	20
1914	Doc Cook	10
1919	Sammy Vick	9
1939	Charlie Keller	7
1967	**Steve Whitaker**	**4**

Most Double Plays

1912	Guy Zinn	1
1914	Doc Cook	2
1919	Sammy Vick	2
1949	Hank Bauer	3
1967	**Steve Whitaker**	**6**

Most Chances Per Game

1912	Guy Zinn	1.8
1919	Sammy Vick	1.9
1939	**Charlie Keller**	**2.1**

Most Total Chances

1912	Guy Zinn	187
1914	Doc Cook	196
1939	**Charlie Keller**	**225**

DID YOU KNOW that when Babe Ruth hit three consecutive home runs for the first time, in 1930, he batted right-handed his fourth time up, swung at and missed two pitches, and then went back to the left side and struck out?

Highest Fielding Percentage

1912	Guy Zinn	.893
1914	Doc Cook	.949
1919	Sammy Vick	.952
1939	Charlie Keller	.969
1967	Steve Whitaker	.982

RECORD HOLDERS LIST

1	Hal Chase	8
1	Hack Simmons	8
1	Neal Ball	8
1	Monte Beville	8
1	Frank Delahanty	8
1	Ray Demmitt	8
1	Guy Zinn	8
1	Frank LaPorte	8
1	Jimmy Austin	8
10	Luke Boone	7
10	Billy Johnson	7
10	Wally Pipp	7
12	Joe DiMaggio	6
12	Tony Lazzeri	6
12	Clyde Engle	6
12	Doc Cook	6
12	Roxy Walters	6
18	Earle Combs	5
18	Truck Hannah	5
18	Charlie Keller	5
21	Red Kleinow	4
21	Jerry Coleman	4
21	Sammy Vick	4
21	Ed Sweeney	4
21	Joe Gedeon	4
27	Johnny Sturm	3
27	Pee Wee Wanninger	3
27	Steve Whitaker	3
27	Phil Rizzuto	3
31	Billy Martin	2
31	Mark Koenig	2
31	Jack Martin	2
31	Tom Tresh	2
31	Muddy Ruel	2
31	Benny Bengough	2
31	Joe Gordon	2
31	Bill Dickey	2
31	Thurmon Munson	2
31	Ira Thomas	2
42	Hank Bauer	1
42	Willie Randolph	1
42	Bobby Brown	1

SUMMARY AND HIGHLIGHTS

Hal Chase was a fine rookie first baseman, but the two who turned in the best job were Wally Pipp and Johnny Sturm.

Pipp was the most active, and he set the putouts and total chances marks, which still have not been broken since 1915.

Johnny Sturm produced the most assists, most double plays, fewest errors, and highest fielding percentage. However, some experts might argue that Pipp's .986 mark in 1915 with the poor gloves was even better than Sturm's average of .990 with a much better glove.

Due to the 162-game schedule, Willie Randolph tallied the most putouts at second base, but even in a 154-game schedule Tony Lazzeri had more assists and total chances.

Jerry Coleman and Billy Martin also had excellent rookie seasons at second base. Coleman is the only second baseman with more than 100 DPs, and Martin committed the fewest errors and possesses the highest fielding percentage.

An interesting mark was set at shortstop, where Neal Ball, the first Yankee rookie, in 1908, fielded more ground balls and had more total chances than any other shortstop. Considering the shorter playing schedule and shabby playing surfaces and rag gloves used in those days, Ball's feat is quite remarkable.

Phil Rizzuto is considered the greatest Yankee shortstop, and he is the only one who took part in more than 100 double plays. Tom Tresh, later to become a fine left fielder, did an excellent job while making the fewest errors and producing the highest fielding percentage.

Billy Johnson was most impressive at the hot corner, Thurmon Munson did the most with the tools of ignorance, and Benny Bengough was brilliant behind the plate, making only three errors. It is a rare occurrence when a player in 1925 establishes a higher fielding percentage than modern players, but that is exactly what Bengough did. His three errors behind the plate produced a .993 fielding percentage, which has never been approached by modern players.

The three most outstanding outfielders were Joe DiMaggio, Earle Combs, and Charlie Keller. Combs is the only outfielder to capture more than 400 fly balls, while also making the fewest errors per chance, even with the miserable gloves of 1925. Combs started and ended his career in center field, while DiMaggio started in left and moved to center and Keller began in right and moved to left field.

When Hal Chase joined the team in 1905, they were still called the Highlanders. He was an utter magician around first base. He was said to possess remarkable grace, speed, and agility. He was the rare combination of left-handed thrower and right-handed batter. "Prince Hal," as he would soon be called, was a pioneer at first base. He played off the bag at a time when this was not commonly done. Charging bunts and throwing runners out at second or third was also a rare practice in those days, but Chase was a master.

BILL DICKEY

This Hall of Fame catcher played a major role as a player and a coach. His six records displayed his superior catching talents, and to this date he still has the most assists of any Yankee catcher.

Bill Dickey is the only catcher with a .300 lifetime batting average.

PHIL RIZZUTO

This gutsy little shortstop would not believe he was too small to play major league baseball. At 5' 6" tall and 150 pounds, the Scooter hung in there with the big boys for 13 marvelous years.

Many believe his fielding abilities and .273 lifetime batting average are superior to some Hall of Fame shortstops.

The Yankees have had exceptional rookies at second base. Such outstanding performers as Tony Lazzeri, Joe Gordon, Jerry Coleman, Billy Martin, and Willie Randolph all put their names into the record book. Joe Gordon was responsible for the Yankees' trading Tony Lazzeri. (Lazzeri was nearing the end of his career.) Gordon was a flashy fielder who developed the nickname "The Flash," and although he was a better-than-average-fielding second baseman, the Yankees were more impressed with his hitting. He slammed 25 home runs as a rookie (second to Joe DiMaggio's 29) and then followed with seasons of 28, 30, 24, 18, 17, and 11 home runs before being traded to Cleveland along with Eddie Bockman for Allie Reynolds. Gordon had four good years with the Indians, as he continued to hit the ball out of the park. He parked 29 for the Tribe in 1947, then added 32, 20, and 19 before calling it quits in 1950.

But the Yankees did extremely well by trading their fabulous second baseman, because Allie Reynolds became a key pitcher in many pennants that would follow. Reynolds, who was part American Indian, had the nickname of "Chief." But when he came to the Yankees and took charge of the pitching staff, he was called "Superchief." In his eight years with the Yankees this fireballing right hander won 131 while losing 60. During that span (1947–54) he was instrumental in six pennants and six World Series championships. Jerry Coleman and Billy Martin also took part in some of those winning seasons.

Willie Randolph became the only rookie second baseman to register more than 300 putouts when he arrived in 1976. Still an active player, Willie will have most of the career records when he retires.

The Yankees had a Pee Wee at shortstop before the Dodgers had Pee Wee Reese. This Pee Wee's name was Wanninger, who set three records in 1925. Two of Wanninger's records were broken by another peewee, although he wasn't called Pee Wee. This 5' 6" 150-pounder was called "Scooter" Rizzuto. Rizzuto was an inspirational member of the Yankees, and he enjoyed a fabulous 13-year career. Despite his size he was an outstanding fielder and a fine contact hitter. His lifetime batting average of .273 is higher than many of the shortstops in the Hall of Fame, but the voters have yet to honor the Scooter.

Bill Dickey and Thurmon Munson were the two greatest rookie catchers (Yogi Berra played only a partial season). Both played their entire careers with the Yankees, with Dickey making the Hall of Fame. Munson's career was cut short by his death in an airplane accident. It was a terrible shock to the baseball world, because Thurmon was one of the league leaders and a hard, hustling player.

Walter Pipp

WALLY PIPP

Wally Pipp is famous for allowing Lou Gehrig to enter the lineup, but he was a marvelous player, as can be seen by his six fabulous fielding records. It took Lou Gehrig 15 years to break five of Pipp's records, and Gehrig could not better Pipp's fielding percentage mark. Pipp was one of the best fielders in Yankee history.

CHAPTER VII

CAREER BATTING RECORDS

BATTING QUIZ
---

1. Only two Yankee players have enjoyed 18-year careers. Do you know them?
2. The most Yankee pinch hits record is held by an outstanding hitting pitcher. Name him.
3. Who had more extra base hits, Babe Ruth or Lou Gehrig?
4. For many years, Hal Chase was the stolen base leader. Who is the new stolen base champion?
5. Can you name the two Yankee players to have more than 8,000 at bats?

DID YOU KNOW that Lou Gehrig broke eight of Babe Ruth's career records?

DID YOU KNOW that if you added the number of walks and strikeouts in Babe Ruth's career, it would make six years of at bats without his hitting the ball?

DID YOU KNOW that two first basemen, Wally Pipp and Lou Gehrig, have set Yankee records for hitting triples?

Most Years

1903–05	Dave Fultz	3
	Ambrose Puttman	3
1904–06	Pat Dougherty	3
1903–07	Clark Griffith	5
	Jimmy Williams	5
1903–08	Wid Conroy	6
1903–09	Jack Chesbro	7
	Kid Elberfeld	7
	Willie Keeler	7
1905–13	Hal Chase	9
1910–18	Ray Caldwell	9
1913–21	Roger Peckinpaugh	9
1915–25	Wally Pipp	11
1916–27	Bob Shawkey	12
1920–34	Babe Ruth	15
1923–39	Lou Gehrig	17
1928–46	Bill Dickey	17
1932–48	Frank Crosetti	17
1946–63	**Yogi Berra**	**18**
1951–68	**Mickey Mantle**	**18**

Most Games

1903–05	Dave Fultz	306
1903–07	Jimmy Williams	685
1903–08	Wid Conroy	797
1903–09	Willie Keeler	873
1905–13	Hal Chase	1,059
1913–21	Roger Peckinpaugh	1,220
1915–25	Wally Pipp	1,488
1920–34	Babe Ruth	2,084
1923–39	Lou Gehrig	2,164
1951–68	**Mickey Mantle**	**2,401**

Most At Bats

1903–05	Dave Fultz	1,056
1903–07	Jimmy Williams	2,536
1903–08	Wid Conroy	3,005
1903–09	Willie Keeler	3,316
1905–13	Hal Chase	4,172
1913–21	Roger Peckinpaugh	4,551
1915–25	Wally Pipp	5,594
1920–34	Babe Ruth	7,217
1923–39	Lou Gehrig	8,001
1951–68	**Mickey Mantle**	**8,102**

* American League Record
** Major League Record
*** Unbroken Major League Record

Most Hits

1903–05	Dave Fultz	257
1903–07	Jimmy Williams	663
1903–08	Wid Conroy	750
1903–09	Willie Keeler	978
1905–13	Hal Chase	1,166
1913–21	Roger Peckinpaugh	1,170
1915–25	Wally Pipp	1,577
1920–34	Babe Ruth	2,518
1923–39	**Lou Gehrig**	**2,721**

Most Singles

1903–05	Dave Fultz	205
1903–07	Jimmy Williams	481
1903–08	Wid Conroy	568
1903–09	Willie Keeler	873
1905–13	Hal Chase	947
1915–25	Wally Pipp	1,117
1920–34	Babe Ruth	1,329
1923–39	**Lou Gehrig**	**1,531**

Most Doubles

1903–05	Dave Fultz	*42
1903–07	Jimmy Williams	123
1905–13	Hal Chase	169
1913–21	Roger Peckinpaugh	174
1915–25	Wally Pipp	259
1920–34	Bob Meusel	338
1920–34	Babe Ruth	424
1923–39	**Lou Gehrig**	**535**

Most Triples

1903–05	Dave Fultz	8
1903–07	Jimmy Williams	45
1903–08	Wid Conroy	59
1908–15	Birdie Cree	62
1915–25	Wally Pipp	121
1924–35	Earle Combs	154
1923–39	**Lou Gehrig**	**162**

Most Home Runs

1903–05	Dave Fultz	2
1903–07	Jimmy Williams	14
1905–13	Hal Chase	22
1913–21	Roger Peckinpaugh	36
1915–25	Wally Pipp	80
1920–29	Bob Meusel	146
1920–34	**Babe Ruth**	****659[1]**

[1] Babe Ruth also hit 49 homers with the Red Sox and 6 with the Braves for a total of 714.

Highest Home Run Percentage

1903–05	Dave Fultz	0.2
1904–06	Pat Dougherty	0.6
1903–07	Jimmy Williams	0.6
1913–21	Roger Peckinpaugh	0.7
1915–25	Wally Pipp	1.4
1920–29	Bob Meusel	2.8
1920–34	**Babe Ruth**	*****9.0**

Most Extra Base Hits

1903–05	Dave Fultz	52
1904–06	Pat Dougherty	53
1903–07	Jimmy Williams	182
1903–08	Wid Conroy	182
1905–13	Hal Chase	239
1913–21	Roger Peckinpaugh	263
1915–25	Wally Pipp	460
1920–29	Bob Meusel	619
1920–34	Babe Ruth	**1,189
1923–39	**Lou Gehrig**	**1,190**

Most Total Bases

1903–05	Dave Fultz	116
1904–06	Pat Dougherty	120
1903–07	Jimmy Williams	437
1903–08	Wid Conroy	443
1905–13	Hal Chase	570
1913–21	Roger Peckinpaugh	651
1915–25	Wally Pipp	1,201
1920–29	Bob Meusel	1,645
1920–34	Babe Ruth	3,838

DID YOU KNOW that in the 13 years Joe DiMaggio played with the Yankees, he was instrumental in helping the team win 11 pennants and nine World Series?

DID YOU KNOW that Roger Maris was so respected as a home run hitter that he was intentionally walked four times in one game in 1962? In that game he also walked unintentionally in his fifth at bat.

DID YOU KNOW that Babe Ruth hit the first home run in Yankee Stadium, in 1923?

Most Runs Scored

1903–05	Dave Fultz	*127
1904–06	Pat Dougherty	140
1903–07	Jimmy Williams	291
1903–08	Wid Conroy	356
1903–09	Willie Keeler	482
1905–13	Hal Chase	550
1913–21	Roger Peckinpaugh	671
1915–25	Wally Pipp	820
1920–29	Bob Meusel	826
1920–34	**Babe Ruth**	**1,959**

Most RBIs

1903–05	Dave Fultz	99
1903–07	Jimmy Williams	206
1905–13	Hal Chase	497
1915–25	Wally Pipp	825
1920–29	Bob Meusel	1,005
1920–34	Babe Ruth	**1,970
1923–39	**Lou Gehrig**	**1,991**

Most Bases on Balls

1903–05	Dave Fultz	88
1903–07	Jimmy Williams	206
1903–09	Willie Keeler	220
1908–15	Birdie Cree	269
1911–16	Roy Hartzell	328
1913–21	Roger Peckinpaugh	508
1920–34	**Babe Ruth**	*****1,847**

Most Strikeouts

1903–12	Statistics Not Kept	
1908–15	Birdie Cree	97
1911–16	Roy Hartzell	118
1913–17	Fritz Maisel	160
1913–21	Roger Peckinpaugh	457
1915–25	Wally Pipp	495
1920–29	Bob Meusel	556
1920–34	Babe Ruth	**1,122
1951–68	**Mickey Mantle**	****1,710**

Most Stolen Bases

1903–05	Dave Fultz	*90
1903–08	Wid Conroy	184
1905–13	Hal Chase	248
1985–88	**Rickey Henderson**	**301[2]**

[2] He is adding to this record each time he steals a base.

Highest Batting Average

1903–05	Dave Fultz	.243
1903–07	Jimmy Williams	.261
1903–09	Willie Keeler	.290
1908–15	Birdie Cree	.292
1922–25	Whitey Witt	.299
1920–29	Bob Meusel	.310
1920–34	**Babe Ruth**	**.349**

Highest Slugging Percentage

1903–05	Dave Fultz	.305
1903–07	Jimmy Williams	.362
1905–13	Harry Wolter	.380
1908–15	Birdie Cree	.398
1918–20	Ping Bodie	.403
1915–25	Wally Pipp	.409
1920–29	Bob Meusel	.495
1920–34	**Babe Ruth**	**•••.703**

Most Pinch At Bats

1903–05	Dave Fultz	12
1906–07	Ira Thomas	18
1905–10	Frank LaPorte	24
1908–11	Charlie Hemphill	37
1910–18	Ray Caldwell	*137
1930–46	**Red Ruffing**	**187**

Most Pinch Hits

1903–05	Dave Fultz	3
1906–08	George Moriarty	3
1905–10	Frank LaPorte	6
1908–11	Charlie Hemphill	7
1908–15	Birdie Cree	9
1910–18	Ray Caldwell	34
1930–46	**Red Ruffing**	**47**

Highest Pinch Batting Average

1903–05	Dave Fultz	.250
1905–10	Frank LaPorte	.250
1908–12	Earl Gardner	.266
1908–15	Birdie Cree	.272
1914–16	Charley Mullen	.333
1920–29	**Bob Meusel**	**.461**

Most Consecutive Games Played

1923–39	Lou Gehrig	•••2,130

Most Grand Slams

1923–39	Lou Gehrig	•••23

RECORD HOLDERS LIST

1	Dave Fultz	20
2	Babe Ruth	16
2	Jimmy Williams	16
4	Wally Pipp	15
5	Hal Chase	12
5	Roger Peckinpaugh	12
7	Lou Gehrig	11
7	Bob Meusel	11
9	Wid Conroy	10
10	Willie Keeler	8
11	Birdie Cree	6
12	Pat Dougherty	5
13	Mickey Mantle	4
14	Frank LaPorte	3
15	Roy Hartzell	2
15	Charlie Hemphill	2
15	Red Ruffing	2
15	Ray Caldwell	2
19	Fritz Maisel	1
19	Ira Thomas	1
19	Earl Gardner	1
19	Charley Mullen	1
19	Whitey Witt	1
19	Yogi Berra	1
19	Ping Bodie	1
19	Harry Wolter	1
19	Rickey Henderson	1

Vic Raschi on Phil Rizzuto: "My best pitch is anything the batter grounds, lines, or pops in the direction of Phil Rizzuto."

SUMMARY AND HIGHLIGHTS

Dave Fultz was the first player to retire from the Yankees with a 3-year career, and this is where the career records begin. Since no records stood before him, Fultz had the privilege of being the record starter.

Fultz's beginning marks were easy for others to break because of the short 3-year time.

Of the everyday players, Jimmy Williams was the first to retire with a 5-year career, and naturally his accomplishments are greater than Fultz's.

As can easily be seen, the big man in career records is the mighty Bambino, who tore up the record book with 16 high-quality records. Seven of these marks are still unbroken.

Prior to Babe Ruth, the man with the big stick was Wally Pipp. Pipp starred from 1915 to 1925 and placed 15 well-earned records in the book. He was the first Yankee to play more than 10 years.

Hal Chase and Roger Peckinpaugh each landed an even dozen marks, but the 11 records set by Lou Gehrig and Bob Meusel are of far higher quality.

Meusel, who retired before the Babe, did his share as a member of Murderers' Row. When he retired, he had more doubles, home runs, a higher home run percentage, more extra base hits, total bases, runs scored, and RBIs than any other Yankee player.

Lou Gehrig did a remarkable job in producing his 11 records because he had to break many of the Babe's marks, since he retired after Ruth. The Iron Horse passed his famous teammate in years and games played, at bats, hits, singles, doubles, triples, extra base hits, and RBIs. And he will go down in history as the man who broke more of Babe Ruth's records than anyone else in the history of baseball!

Two modern greats, Mickey Mantle and Yogi Berra, share the mark for most years, and Mantle, even with his physical handicaps, played more games and had more at bats than any other Yankee.

It took Hal Chase 9 years to steal 248 bases, a record that was good enough to last 75 years. But it took Rickey Henderson only 3 years and 1 month to break it. At this writing Henderson has broken the record and is on his way to setting the Major League's greatest stolen base mark.

One of the most unlikely records is found in the pinch hitting department. Red Ruffing, a pitcher, has held the pinch at bats and pinch hit marks for 40 years! Bob Meusel's .461 pinch batting average is by far the best.

Yogi Berra and Mickey Mantle are the only two Yankee heros who put on the proud pinstripes for 18 years. What is most remarkable about Mantle's career is that he freely admits that he did not take care of himself and that he could have played more years if he had. On the other hand, Yogi Berra toiled away most of his career behind the plate but got some relief from Elston Howard during the last few years.

Yogi surprised the baseball world in 1946 and under the guidance of Bill Dickey became a better catcher than most people thought he could possibly

BABE RUTH
Forty-eight percent of his records are still unbroken.

RECORD PROFILE
BABE RUTH
1920–1934

Most Years Played	15	5 years before broken
Most Games Played	2,084	5 years before broken
Most At Bats	7,217	5 years before broken
Most Hits	2,518	5 years before broken
Most Singles	1,329	5 years before broken
Most Doubles	424	5 years before broken
Most Home Runs	659	**NEVER BROKEN**
Highest Home Run Percentage	9.0	**NEVER BROKEN**
Most Runs Scored	1,959	**NEVER BROKEN**
Most RBIs	1,970	5 years before broken
Most Bases on Balls	1,847	**NEVER BROKEN**
Highest Batting Average	.349	**NEVER BROKEN**
Highest Slugging Percentage	.703	**NEVER BROKEN**
Most Extra Base Hits	1,189	5 years before broken
Most Total Bases	3,838	**NEVER BROKEN**
Most Strikeouts	1,122	34 years before broken

be. He got so good at it that in 1958 he handled 550 chances without making an error, thus becoming one of the few catchers to do that.

Yogi was a great hitter, although a very unusual one. He had the biggest strike zone of any player in baseball. His theory was that if he could reach it, he could and would hit it. He did not ask himself if the pitch was a ball or a strike before committing to it. If he could reach it and it was outside, he would drive it to left field (he was a left-handed hitter). If the pitch was inside, low or high, Yogi would belt it to right field. So good was Yogi at hitting the baseball that when he retired in 1965, he had hit more home runs than any other catcher. (Johnny Bench has since passed him, but Yogi is still the American League champion.)

During his exciting career, which saw him participate in 14 pennants and World Series, the fabulous Yogi, who is now famous for saying, "It ain't over till it's over," accumulated 33 marvelous records. Yogi has five American League marks (three tied but unbroken), five Major League records (three tied but unbroken), 12 World Series records (five unbroken, one tied), and 11 Yankee club marks (ten unbroken, one tied).

Yogi can be proud of the fact that he played the most World Series games and has the most at bats, most hits, and most singles and is tied for most doubles.

A little-known aspect of Berra's career is that during his 18 years of play he led the league in various fielding categories a whopping 30 times! The record for being a league leader in fielding is 32, held by the great Cap Anson. Yogi is second on this list.

Mickey Mantle will easily go down in history as the greatest switch hitter. He could hit home runs from both sides of the plate with ease, and his blinding speed made him an outstanding centerfielder.

When Mickey hit the Big Apple, he was asked to fill the shoes of the great Joltin' Joe DiMaggio. Mantle filled them and then some. His 18 years of play enabled him to play more games and gather more at bats than any other Yankee. As great as he was, it was difficult for him to break records, because he had to do better than Babe Ruth, Lou Gehrig, Joe DiMaggio, and Yogi Berra. Nevertheless, the "Commerce Comet" put 24 records in the book. Mickey has one American League and one Major League record. He also has one All-Star game record, but where he really excels is in World Series records. The Mick has ten World Series marks, seven of which are still unbroken. No other player has hit as many home runs, scored more runs, or had more RBIs, total bases, extra base hits, bases on balls, or strikeouts in World Series play than he. In addition, Mickey has put together 11 Yankee club records, of which seven remain unbroken.

Sandwiched between Babe Ruth and Lou Gehrig, and Yogi Berra and Mickey Mantle, was the Yankee Clipper, Joe DiMaggio. Joe D. was easily the most graceful of all Yankees, and his long, loping strides ate up the center field pasture as he time and again hauled in long drives up the left center field gap. I can still see him backhanding those balls and making it look so

LOU GEHRIG

Was part of the greatest one-two slugging combination in baseball history.

RECORD PROFILE
LOU GEHRIG
1923–1939

Most Years Played	17	7 years before broken
Most Games Played	2,164	29 years before broken
Consecutive Games Played	2,130	**NEVER BROKEN**
Most At Bats	8,001	29 years before broken
Most Hits	2,721	**NEVER BROKEN**
Most Singles	1,531	**NEVER BROKEN**
Most Doubles	535	**NEVER BROKEN**
Most Triples	162	**NEVER BROKEN**
Most RBIs	1,991	**NEVER BROKEN**
Most Extra Base Hits	1,190	**NEVER BROKEN**
Most Grand Slams	23	**NEVER BROKEN**

Has more unbroken records than any other New York Yankee.

very routine. Moreover, DiMag had a marvelous throwing arm. It has been said that when line drives were hit to him, he threw the ball back on a line that was harder than the ball going out.

Everyone knows what a first-class hitter he was, and hitting in the clutch and under pressure, Joltin' Joe proved his great talent by hitting in 56 consecutive games. Some people say that was the most exciting spectacle in baseball history. A 44-game streak (the previous record) is quite a feat, but Joe broke that and kept on going. He was front-page news every day until Ken Keltner, third baseman for the Cleveland Indians, made his fame by stopping two hard smashes off DiMaggio's bat to break his streak.

Often overlooked about DiMaggio's talents was his great base-running ability. He turned many of his singles into doubles by smartly cutting the angle at the first base bag and with his long and quick strides made it safely into second base with a beautiful hook slide. (You don't see many hook slides today.) It was seldom that he made a wrong judgment on the bases, and when he went for a base he usually made it.

During his spectacular career Joe DiMaggio was expected to carry on in the tradition that Ruth and Gehrig had built, and the young man from San Francisco, son of Italian immigrants, did just that and more. He was the leader of the world champions in such a quiet and unassuming manner that his presence could be felt without his uttering a word.

In his 13 years of play the Yankee Clipper put together 60 records of high quality. He had six American League (two unbroken, two tied), four Major League (one unbroken, two tied), seven All-Star game (all broken), 11 World Series (four unbroken, one tied), and 32 Yankee club records of which 21 remain unbroken.

Joe DiMaggio was a complete player, a master at every part of the game. Five times he was a fielding leader, and he was one of the few players to win the MVP award three times. He became a Hall of Famer in 1955.

CHAPTER VIII

CAREER PITCHING RECORDS

PITCHING QUIZ

1. Can you name the Yankee pitcher who has the highest winning percentage?
2. One of the best Yankee pitchers walked the most batters. Name him.
3. Who is the all-time Yankee strikeout leader?
4. This pitcher belted 31 home runs, a mark that still stands after 41 years. Do you know him?
5. Name the relief pitcher who has the most wins.

DID YOU KNOW that Red Ruffing batted over .300 six times?

DID YOU KNOW that Whitey Ford is the only pitcher to have a 16-year career?

DID YOU KNOW that Russ Ford's 2.53 ERA record was set in 1913 and has yet to be broken?

Most Years

1903–04	Bill Wolfe	2
1903–05	Ambrose Puttman	3
1903–07	Clark Griffith	5
1903–09	Jack Chesbro	7
1908–15	Jack Warhop	8
1910–17	Ray Fisher	8
1910–18	Ray Caldwell	9
1915–27	Bob Shawkey	13
1930–42	Lefty Gomez	13
1930–46	Red Ruffing	15
1950–67	**Whitey Ford**	**16**

Most Appearances

1903	Jesse Tannehill	32
1903–07	Clark Griffith	87
1903–09	Jack Chesbro	*269
1915–27	Bob Shawkey	448
1930–46	Red Ruffing	464
1950–67	**Whitey Ford**	**498**

Most Starts

1903	Jesse Tannehill	31
1903–07	Clark Griffith	44
1903–09	Jack Chesbro	223
1915–27	Bob Shawkey	303
1930–42	Lefty Gomez	320
1930–46	Red Ruffing	428
1950–67	**Whitey Ford**	**438**

Most Complete Games

1903	Jesse Tannehill	22
1903–07	Clark Griffith	35
1903–09	Jack Chesbro	167
1915–27	Bob Shawkey	168
1930–42	Lefty Gomez	173
1930–46	**Red Ruffing**	**262**

Most Wins

1903	Jesse Tannehill	15
1903–07	Clark Griffith	32
1903–09	Jack Chesbro	*128
1915–27	Bob Shawkey	168
1930–42	Lefty Gomez	189
1930–46	Red Ruffing	231
1950–67	**Whitey Ford**	**236**

* American League Record
** Major League Record
*** Unbroken Major League Record

Most Losses

1903	Jesse Tannehill	15
1903–04	Bill Wolfe	18
1903–07	Clark Griffith	23
1903–09	Jack Chesbro	89
1908–15	Jack Warhop	94
1910–18	Ray Caldwell	99
1915–27	**Bob Shawkey**	**131**

Highest Winning Percentage
(Minimum 3 Years)

1903–07	Clark Griffith	.581
1903–09	Jack Chesbro	.589
1921–30	Waite Hoyt	.613
1923–33	Herb Pennock	.642
1930–42	Lefty Gomez	.649
1937–47	**Spud Chandler**	**.717**

Lowest ERA (Minimum 3 Years)

1903–07	Clark Griffith	2.57
1903–09	Jack Chesbro	2.54
1909–13	**Russ Ford**	**2.53**

Most Innings

1903	Jesse Tannehill	240
1903–07	Clark Griffith	697
1903–09	Jack Chesbro	1,953
1915–27	Bob Shawkey	2,489
1930–42	Lefty Gomez	2,498
1930–46	Red Ruffing	3,169
1950–67	**Whitey Ford**	**3,170**

Lefty Gomez after being asked how far a batter's home run off him had traveled: "I don't know, but it took someone 45 minutes to fetch it."

Waite Hoyt on the secret of pitching success: "Get a job with the Yankees." (After two seasons with the Red Sox showing ten wins, he was traded to New York and won 157 games in 9 years.)

Most Hits Allowed

1903	Jesse Tannehill	258
1903–07	Clark Griffith	447
1903–09	Jack Chesbro	1,677
1915–27	Bob Shawkey	2,407
1923–33	Herb Pennock	2,471
1930–46	**Red Ruffing**	**3,037**

Most Bases on Balls

1903	Jesse Tannehill	34
1903–07	Clark Griffith	85
1903–09	Jack Chesbro	421
1910–18	Ray Caldwell	576
1915–27	Bob Shawkey	855
1930–42	**Lefty Gomez**	**1,090**

Most Strikeouts

1903	Jesse Tannehill	106
1903–07	Clark Griffith	172
1903–09	Jack Chesbro	*913
1915–27	Bob Shawkey	1,163
1930–42	Lefty Gomez	1,468
1930–46	Red Ruffing	1,526
1950–67	**Whitey Ford**	**1,956**

Most Shutouts

1903	Jesse Tannehill	2
1903–07	Clark Griffith	6
1903–09	Jack Chesbro	18
1915–27	Bob Shawkey	26
1930–42	Lefty Gomez	26
1930–46	Red Ruffing	37
1950–67	**Whitey Ford**	**45**

RELIEF PITCHING RECORDS

Most Appearances

1903	Snake Wiltse	1
	Jesse Tannehill	1
	Doc Adkins	1
1903–04	Bill Wolfe	9
1903–05	Ambrose Puttman	15
	Jake Powell	15
1903–07	Clark Griffith	*43
1908–15	Jack Warhop	71
1909–21	Jack Quinn	84
1915–27	Bob Shawkey	139
1927–33	Wilcy Moore	146
1932–46	Johnny Murphy	*343
1972–78	**Sparky Lyle**	**420**

Most Wins

1903	Snake Wiltse	1
1903–05	Jake Powell	3
1903–07	Clark Griffith	7
1905–08	Bill Hogg	7
1903–09	Jack Chesbro	*10
1908–15	Jack Warhop	13
1909–21	Jack Quinn	20
1915–27	Bob Shawkey	28
1927–33	Wilcy Moore	29
1932–46	**Johnny Murphy**	****73**

Most Losses

1903–05	Jake Powell	2
1903–07	Clark Griffith	6
1903–09	Jack Chesbro	6
1904–09	Al Orth	6
1909–15	Jack Warhop	15
1915–27	Bob Shawkey	20
1932–46	**Johnny Murphy**	****42**

Most Saves

1903	Doc Adkins	1
1903–05	Jake Powell	*3
1903–07	Clark Griffith	6
1908–15	Jack Warhop	8
1915–19	Allan Russell	11
1920–23	Carl Mays	11
1915–27	Bob Shawkey	26
1921–30	Waite Hoyt	28
1927–33	Wilcy Moore	**43
1932–46	Johnny Murphy	**104
1972–78	**Sparky Lyle**	**141**

Most Wins Plus Saves

1903	Snake Wiltse	1
	Doc Adkins	1
1903–05	Jake Powell	6
1903–07	Clark Griffith	13
1908–15	Jack Warhop	20
1915–19	Allan Russell	21
1909–21	Jack Quinn	26
1915–27	Bob Shawkey	54
1927–33	Wilcy Moore	**72
1932–46	Johnny Murphy	**177
1972–78	**Sparky Lyle**	**198**

Highest Winning Percentage
(Minimum 50 Games)

1908–15	Jack Warhop	.464
1909–21	Jack Quinn	.829

Lowest ERA
(Minimum 50 Games)

1908–15	Jack Warhop	3.09
1915–27	Bob Shawkey	3.09
1958–60	Ryne Duren	2.95
1966–68	Dooley Womack	2.75
1969–72	Jack Aker	2.60
1972–78	Sparky Lyle	2.44
1978–83	Goose Gossage	2.03

Most Innings

1903–07	Clark Griffith	138
1908–15	Jack Warhop	265
1915–27	Bob Shawkey	350
1932–46	Johnny Murphy	710
1972–78	Sparky Lyle	746

Most Hits Allowed

1903–07	Clark Griffith	100
1908–15	Jack Warhop	223
1915–27	Bob Shawkey	327
1932–46	Johnny Murphy	660
1972–78	Sparky Lyle	666

Most Bases on Balls

1903–07	Clark Griffith	17
1908–15	Jack Warhop	80
1915–27	Bob Shawkey	96
1932–46	Johnny Murphy	311
1944–50	Joe Page	319

Most Strikeouts

1903–07	Clark Griffith	26
1908–15	Jack Warhop	83
1915–27	Bob Shawkey	115
1932–46	Johnny Murphy	246
1944–50	Joe Page	412
1972–78	Sparky Lyle	454
1978–83	Goose Gossage	506

DID YOU KNOW that the Yankees wore the pinstripes for the first time in 1915?

PITCHERS CAREER BATTING RECORDS

Most At Bats

1903–07	Clark Griffith	163
1903–09	Jack Chesbro	745
1910–18	Ray Caldwell	951
1930–46	Red Ruffing	1,486

Most Hits

1903–07	Clark Griffith	26
1903–09	Jack Chesbro	144
1910–18	Ray Caldwell	238
1930–46	Red Ruffing	401

Most Home Runs

1903–07	Clark Griffith	1
1903–09	Jack Chesbro	4
1910–18	Ray Caldwell	7
1930–46	Red Ruffing	31

Highest Batting Average

1903–07	Clark Griffith	.159
1903–09	Jack Chesbro	.193
1910–18	Ray Caldwell	.250
1930–46	Red Ruffing	.268

Most Times Batted Over .300

1921–30	Waite Hoyt	1
1930–46	Red Ruffing	6

RECORD HOLDERS LIST

1	Clark Griffith	21
1	Bob Shawkey	21
3	Jack Chesbro	14
4	Jack Warhop	13
5	Jesse Tannehill	11
6	Johnny Murphy	9
6	Red Ruffing	9
6	Lefty Gomez	9
9	Whitey Ford	7
9	Sparky Lyle	7
11	Jake Powell	5
12	Jack Quinn	4
12	Wilcy Moore	4
14	Doc Adkins	3
14	Snake Wiltse	3
16	Goose Gossage	2
16	Joe Page	2

16	Bill Wolfe	2	22	Bill Hogg	1
16	Herb Pennock	2	22	Al Orth	1
16	Ambrose Puttman	2	22	Allan Russell	1
16	Waite Hoyt	2	22	Carl Mays	1
22	Ray Fisher	1	22	Ryne Duren	1
22	Spud Chandler	1	22	Dooley Womack	1
22	Russ Ford	1	22	Jack Aker	1

SUMMARY AND HIGHLIGHTS

Many of the above records do not truly represent pitchers' talents. It must be remembered that records must have a starting point, and some of the beginning records lack quality and should only be treated as the starting points.

Records and players' greatness should be judged by the number of years each record lasted and the value of the records. The negative marks such as bases on balls and hits allowed should count against a player's evaluations.

Griffith, Shawkey, Chesbro, and Warhop are high on the list due to a combination of good work and longevity plus being involved in many of the beginning records.

Jack Chesbro was the first superstar starting pitcher, although he had already posted good numbers in his four years with Pittsburgh. Bob Shawkey was the next outstanding starting pitcher, and he was followed by Lefty Gomez, Red Ruffing, and Whitey Ford.

Shawkey was the first to appear in more than 400 games, pitch 2,000 innings, and strike out more than 1,000 batters.

Lefty Gomez improved nine of the starting pitchers' records and has one of the highest winning percentages on the pitching staff.

Prior to Whitey Ford, Red Ruffing was the most active pitcher in Yankee history. He was the first to complete a 15-year career, was the first to win more than 200 games, and leads the club in complete games.

Whitey Ford is considered the greatest pitcher in New York Yankee history, and the reason can easily be seen in the seven records he created. Whitey pitched the most years and appeared in the most games, and has the most starts, most wins, most innings, most strikeouts, and most shutouts.

Spud Chandler has the highest winning percentage for pitchers with fewer than 200 wins, while Whitey Ford is number one among those with more than 200 wins. Ford's total of 236 wins against 106 losses represents a brilliant .690 winning percentage, the highest of any pitcher in the Hall of Fame.

Whitey spent his entire 16-year career with the Yankees, during which time he led the league 15 times in various pitching departments. He was instrumental in leading the club to 11 pennants and World Series. As a result of participating in 11 World Series, the curve-balling left-hander has the most World Series wins, losses, games started, innings, hits, walks, and strikeouts.

A complete tabulation of Ford's records indicates that the smooth lefty established a total of 33 magnificent records. He had two American League and one Major League record, four All-Star game marks (two unbroken, two tied), and 15 World Series records (ten unbroken, four tied). Whitey accumulated 11 Yankee club records, and nine of them are still unbroken.

Since the method of pitching has changed so drastically, the career of the first great Yankee pitcher should be examined more closely. Jack Chesbro began his career in 1899 with Pittsburgh of the National League. After getting off to a slow start (20 wins over two seasons), the stout right-hander won 20 or more games 5 out of the next 6 years. He came to the Yankees in 1903 after having successful seasons of 21 and 28 wins with Pittsburgh.

In 1902 Happy Jack was happier than ever, because he started 33 games, completed 31, won 28, and lost only six. Eight wins were shutouts, and he ended the season with a fine 2.17 ERA. Chesbro's most exciting year came in 1904, when the Yankees were still called the Highlanders. His 41 wins created a record that no American League pitcher has come close to breaking.

Chesbro took the mound for 11 years and won a total of 198 while taking it on the chin 132 times. His ERA was a smart 2.68, and he spun 35 shutouts. Fourteen times he was a league leader in various pitching departments, which resulted in 57 records. Of these marks, he had one National League and 18 American League records. Three of his American League records still stand. While a Yankee, the hardworking righty accumulated 38 club records, the most of any Yankee pitcher. Five of these marks remain unbroken.

Red Ruffing had a very unusual and exciting career. He got off to a horrible start with the Boston Red Sox. Bob Shawkey, a fine Yankee pitcher and at the time the team manager, asked team General Manager Ed Barrow to purchase Ruffing's contract from the Red Sox because he had spotted a flaw in Ruffing's mechanics that he was confident if corrected would turn the big right-hander into a winning pitcher. The Red Sox were glad to get rid of Ruffing, who had compiled a losing record of 39 wins and 96 losses. And when the Yankees offered Cedric Durst and $50,000 cash, the Red Sox jumped at the offer. But Shawkey knew what he had to do to make Ruffing a winning pitcher, and what he did helped the Yankees to numerous pennants and World Series victories. In Ruffing's 15 years with the Yankees he won 231 games while losing only 129. No other pitcher has gotten off to as bad a beginning and ended up in the Hall of Fame.

But Ruffing's pitching wasn't the only remarkable thing about his career. He will probably go down in baseball history as the game's greatest hitting pitcher. So good was he that he was often used as the club's number-one pinch hitter. In fact, to this day he still holds the Yankee club record for most career pinch hits! When he was on the mound, he gave the Yankees nine good hitters in the lineup. He batted over .300 six times with the Yankees and twice with the Red Sox. His 31 career home runs, 401 hits, and .268 lifetime batting average are all Yankee pitcher records.

In all, Red Ruffing put together 27 records, of which one rests in the American League, three are All-Star game marks, seven are World Series records (one unbroken, two tied), and 16 are Yankee club records (six unbroken).

In the relief pitching department, Snake Wiltse was the first to win a

SPARKY LYLE

His 420 games in relief are the most of any New York Yankee relief pitcher.

Lyle's combination of 198 wins plus saves is also a club record, as are his 141 saves and 746 innings pitched.

Sparky spun an impressive 2.44 ERA and struck out 454 batters, which were also club records until Goose Gossage posted a brilliant 2.03 ERA and 506 strikeouts.

RED RUFFING
Best-hitting pitcher in New York Yankee history.

RECORD PROFILE
RED RUFFING
1930–1946
CAREER PITCHING AND BATTING RECORDS

Most Years	15	21 years before broken
Most Appearances	464	21 years before broken
Most Starts	428	21 years before broken
Most Complete Games	262	**NEVER BROKEN**
Most Wins	231	21 years before broken
Most Innings	3,169	21 years before broken
Most Hits Allowed	3,037	**NEVER BROKEN**
Most Strikeouts	1,526	21 years before broken
Most Shutouts	37	21 years before broken
Most Pinch At Bats	187	**NEVER BROKEN**
Most Pinch Hits	47	**NEVER BROKEN**
Most At Bats by a Pitcher	1,486	**NEVER BROKEN**
Most Hits by a Pitcher	401	**NEVER BROKEN**
Most Home Runs by a Pitcher	31	**NEVER BROKEN**
Highest Batting Average by a Pitcher	.268	**NEVER BROKEN**
Most Times Over .300 by a Pitcher	6	**NEVER BROKEN**

WHITEY FORD
The greatest pitcher in New York Yankee history.

RECORD PROFILE
WHITEY FORD
1950–1967
CAREER PITCHING RECORDS

Most Years	16	NEVER BROKEN
Most Appearances	498	NEVER BROKEN
Most Starts	438	NEVER BROKEN
Most Wins	236	NEVER BROKEN
Most Innings	3,170	NEVER BROKEN
Most Strikeouts	1,956	NEVER BROKEN
Most Shutouts	45	NEVER BROKEN

Has the most unbroken records of any New York Yankee pitcher.

game in 1903. Powell, Griffith, Hogg, and Chesbro extended this category, and Jack Warhop was the first reliever to win more than ten games. He was also the first to work in more than 50 games; thus most of the relief pitching marks begin with him.

Jack Quinn and Bob Shawkey pitched both as starters and in the bullpen and improved many of the relief pitching records.

Wilcy Moore was considered the first super relief pitcher when he starred from 1927 to 1933. He was the first to win 30 games and reach the 60 wins plus saves level.

Johnny Murphy succeeded Moore as the next relief ace, and he was followed by Fireman Joe Page. But the two greatest Yankee relievers were Sparky Lyle and Goose Gossage, who would follow. Modern-day ace Dave Righetti is fast closing in on these two and should soon have his name alongside them in the record book.

At this date Lyle has appeared in the most games and is second in wins but first in saves and wins plus saves. Gossage has been the toughest to score on, as is indicated by the 2.03 ERA he posted while with the Yankees. Gossage left the Yankees as a free agent in 1984, which prompted the front office to convert Dave Righetti from their ace starting pitcher into their ace relief pitcher. So far this has been a stroke of genius, as big Dave has successfully met the challenge and has never saved fewer than 30 games per year.

CHAPTER IX

CAREER FIELDING RECORDS

FIELDING QUIZ

1. Can you name the Yankee shortstop who has five unbroken records?
2. This marvelous Yankee centerfielder established eight records, of which four still stand today. Name him.
3. Name the Yankee leftfielder who holds four records that are 50 or more years old.
4. Can you name the Yankee catcher who has the most records?
5. Which Yankee shortstop has the highest fielding percentage?

DID YOU KNOW that Don Mattingly already claims two fielding marks at first base?

DID YOU KNOW that Ted Williams once said about Phil Rizzuto, "If we had had him, the Boston Red Sox would have won all those pennants and World Series"?

FIRST BASE

Most Putouts

1903–04	John Ganzel	2,638
1905–13	Hal Chase	*9,831
1915–25	Wally Pipp	14,772
1923–39	Lou Gehrig	*19,510

Most Assists

1903–04	John Ganzel	157
1905–13	Hal Chase	577
1915–25	Wally Pipp	912
1923–39	Lou Gehrig	1,079

Most Errors

1903–04	John Ganzel	34
1905–13	Hal Chase	239

Fewest Errors Per Year
(Minimum 5 Years)

1905–13	Hal Chase	29.9
1915–25	Wally Pipp	13.8
1923–39	Lou Gehrig	13.3
1954–62	Bill Skowron	8.2
1963–69	Joe Pepitone	8.0
1983–88	Don Mattingly	6.4

Most Double Plays

1903–04	John Ganzel	117
1905–13	Hal Chase	434
1915–25	Wally Pipp	949
1923–39	Lou Gehrig	*1,574

Most Chances Per Game

1903–04	John Ganzel	11.4

Most Total Chances

1903–04	John Ganzel	2,829
1905–13	Hal Chase	10,647
1915–25	Wally Pipp	15,822
1923–39	Lou Gehrig	*20,790

Highest Fielding Percentage

1903–04	John Ganzel	.980
1915–25	Wally Pipp	.991
1923–39	Lou Gehrig	.991
1954–62	Bill Skowron	.993
1963–69	Joe Pepitone	.994
1983–88	Don Mattingly	.995

SECOND BASE

Most Putouts

1903–07	Jimmy Williams	*1,609
1926–37	Tony Lazzeri	3,305
1976–88	Willie Randolph	3,982

Most Assists

1903–07	Jimmy Williams	*2,040
1921–25	Aaron Ward	2,088
1926–37	Tony Lazzeri	4,392
1976–88	Willie Randolph	4,996

Most Errors

1903–07	Jimmy Williams	*155
1926–37	Tony Lazzeri	257

Fewest Errors Per Year
(Minimum 5 Years)

1903–07	Jimmy Williams	31.0
1921–25	Aaron Ward	21.2
1957–66	Bobby Richardson	15.5
1967–73	Horace Clarke	14.1

Most Double Plays

1903–07	Jimmy Williams	*241
1921–25	Aaron Ward	311
1926–37	Tony Lazzeri	797
1957–66	Bobby Richardson	960
1976–88	Willie Randolph	1,233

DID YOU KNOW that Enos Slaughter cried when he was traded to the Yankees in 1954? But his American League opponents cried during the next four years, in which Slaughter helped the Yankees win four pennants.

Most Chances Per Game

1903–07	Jimmy Williams	*5.6
1921–25	Aaron Ward	5.7

Most Total Chances

1903–07	Jimmy Williams	*5,500
1926–37	Tony Lazzeri	7,954
1976–88	Willie Randolph	9,161

Highest Fielding Percentage

1903–07	Jimmy Williams	*.955
1918–20	Del Pratt	.970
1921–25	Aaron Ward	.971
1957–66	Bobby Richardson	.978
1967–73	Horace Clarke	.983

SHORTSTOP

Most Putouts

1903–07	Kid Elberfeld	1,177
1913–21	Roger Peckinpaugh	2,336
1932–48	Frank Crosetti	2,807

Most Assists

1903–07	Kid Elberfeld	1,757
1913–21	Roger Peckinpaugh	3,660
1932–48	Frank Crosetti	4,149

Most Errors

1903–07	Kid Elberfeld	247
1913–21	Roger Peckinpaugh	324
1932–48	Frank Crosetti	862

Fewest Errors Per Year
(Minimum 5 Years)

1903–07	Kid Elberfeld	49.4
1913–21	Roger Peckinpaugh	36.0
1932–48	Frank Crosetti	30.0
1941–54	Phil Rizzuto	22.4
1957–65	Tony Kubek	17.2
1977–81	Bucky Dent	13.6

Most Double Plays

1903–07	Kid Elberfeld	168
1913–21	Roger Peckinpaugh	*502
1932–48	Frank Crosetti	862

Most Chances Per Game

1903–07	Kid Elberfeld	5.9

Most Total Chances

1903–07	Kid Elberfeld	3,181
1913–21	Roger Peckinpaugh	6,320
1932–48	Frank Crosetti	7,328

Highest Fielding Percentage

1903–07	Kid Elberfeld	.922
1913–21	Roger Peckinpaugh	.949
1922–24	Everett Scott	.964
1941–54	Phil Rizzuto	.968
1977–81	Bucky Dent	.977

THIRD BASE

Most Putouts

1903–08	Wid Conroy	569
1916–20	Frank Baker	770
1922–28	Joe Dugan	811
1931–42	Red Rolfe	1,304

Most Assists

1903–08	Wid Conroy	912
1916–20	Frank Baker	1,268
1922–28	Joe Dugan	1,406
1931–42	Red Rolfe	2,231
1973–83	Graig Nettles	3,459

Most Errors

1903–08	Wid Conroy	86
1916–20	Frank Baker	96
1931–42	Red Rolfe	166
1973–83	Graig Nettles	181

Fewest Errors Per Year
(Minimum 5 Years)

1903–08	Wid Conroy	17.2
1922–28	Joe Dugan	15.1

Most Double Plays

1903–08	Wid Conroy	31
1916–20	Frank Baker	111
1922–28	Joe Dugan	117
1931–42	Red Rolfe	210
1960–66	Clete Boyer	219
1973–83	Graig Nettles	293

Most Chances Per Game

1903–08	Wid Conroy	3.6
1916–20	Frank Baker	3.6
1960–66	Clete Boyer	3.6

Most Total Chances

1903–08	Wid Conroy	1,567
1916–20	Frank Baker	2,134
1922–28	Joe Dugan	2,308
1931–42	Red Rolfe	3,701
1973–83	**Graig Nettles**	**4,799**

Highest Fielding Percentage

1903–08	Wid Conroy	.934
1916–20	Frank Baker	.955
1922–28	Joe Dugan	*.959
1954–58	Andy Carey	.961
1960–66	**Clete Boyer**	**.965**

CATCHING

Most Putouts

1903	Monte Beville	296
1904–05	Deacon McGuire	896
1904–09	Red Kleinow	1,960
1909–14	Ed Sweeney	2,484
1928–46	Bill Dickey	**7,965
1946–63	**Yogi Berra**	****8,711**

Most Assists

1903	Monte Beville	66
1904–05	Deacon McGuire	189
1904–09	Red Kleinow	546
1909–14	Ed Sweeney	750
1928–46	**Bill Dickey**	**942**

Most Errors

1903	Monte Beville	15
1904–05	Deacon McGuire	31
1904–09	Red Kleinow	78
1909–14	**Ed Sweeney**	**121**

Fewest Errors Per Year
(Minimum 5 Years)

1904–09	Red Kleinow	13.0
1928–46	Bill Dickey	8.0
1946–63	Yogi Berra	7.8
1961–67	**Elston Howard**	**5.1**

* Indicates an American League record.
** Indicates a Major League record.
*** Indicates an unbroken Major League record.

Most Double Plays

1903	Jack O'Connor	6
1904–05	Deacon McGuire	15
1904–09	Red Kleinow	33
1909–14	Ed Sweeney	42
1921–25	Wally Schang	48
1928–46	Bill Dickey	137
1946–63	**Yogi Berra**	**175**

Most Chances Per Game

1903	Jack O'Connor	5.4
1904–05	**Deacon McGuire**	**6.6**

Most Total Chances

1903	Monte Beville	377
1904–05	Deacon McGuire	1,116
1904–09	Red Kleinow	2,584
1909–14	Ed Sweeney	3,355
1928–46	Bill Dickey	9,047
1946–63	**Yogi Berra**	****9,619**

Highest Fielding Percentage
(Minimum 5 Years)

1904–09	Red Kleinow	*.969
1921–25	Wally Schang	.972
1928–46	Bill Dickey	*.988
1946–63	Yogi Berra	.988
1960–67	**Elston Howard**	***991**

DID YOU KNOW that home plate was originally 12″ wide and was changed to 17″ in 1900?

DID YOU KNOW that from 1885 to 1893 a portion of the bat could be flat on one side? (It was supposed to be helpful in laying down bunts.)

DID YOU KNOW that rookie pitcher Russ Van Atta belted four singles in the very first game he pitched—and it tied a record set by Casey Stengel? Van Atta did it in 1933, and Casey was charmed in 1912.

LEFT FIELD			CENTER FIELD		
Most Putouts			*Most Putouts*		
1903	Lefty Davis	176	1903–05	Dave Fultz	502
1904–05	Pat Dougherty	308	1908–11	Charlie Hemphill	614
1910–13	Birdie Cree	686	1922–24	Whitey Witt	1,031
1920–29	Bob Meusel	1,632	1925–33	Earle Combs	2,874
1965–79	Roy White	3,222	1936–51	Joe DiMaggio	4,177
			1951–68	Mickey Mantle	4,273
Most Assists					
1903	Lefty Davis	7	*Most Assists*		
1904–05	Pat Dougherty	25	1903–05	Dave Fultz	33
1910–13	Birdie Cree	47	1908–11	Charlie Hemphill	33
1920–29	Bob Meusel	87	1922–24	Whitey Witt	34
			1925–33	Earle Combs	61
Most Errors			1936–51	Joe DiMaggio	133
1903	Lefty Davis	19			
1904–05	Pat Dougherty	33	*Most Errors*		
1920–29	Bob Meusel	66	1903–05	Dave Fultz	26
			1908–11	Charlie Hemphill	32
Fewest Errors Per Year			1925–33	Earle Combs	84
(Minimum 5 Years)			1936–51	Joe DiMaggio	97
1920–29	Bob Meusel	9.4			
1939–49	Charlie Keller	5.4	*Fewest Errors Per Year*		
1949–54	Gene Woodling	2.4	*(Minimum 5 Years)*		
			1925–33	Earle Combs	9.3
			1936–51	Joe DiMaggio	8.0
Most Double Plays			1951–68	Mickey Mantle	6.5
1903	Lefty Davis	1			
1904–05	Pat Dougherty	3	*Most Chances Per Game*		
1920–29	Bob Meusel	22	1903–05	Dave Fultz	2.3
			1919–20	Ping Bodie	2.3
Most Chances Per Game			1918–21	Eddie Miller	2.5
1903	Lefty Davis	2.0	1922–24	Whitey Witt	2.6
1920–29	Bob Meusel	2.1	1925–33	Earle Combs	2.7
1939–49	Charlie Keller	2.2	1936–51	Joe DiMaggio	2.8
Most Total Chances			*Most Total Chances*		
1903	Lefty Davis	202	1903–05	Dave Fultz	561
1904–05	Pat Dougherty	466	1908–11	Charlie Hemphill	679
1910–13	Birdie Cree	763	1922–24	Whitey Witt	1,090
1920–29	Bob Meusel	1,785	1925–33	Earle Combs	3,019
1965–79	Roy White	3,345	1936–51	Joe DiMaggio	4,407
			1951–68	Mickey Mantle	4,460
Highest Fielding Percentage					
1903	Lefty Davis	.906	*Most Double Plays*		
1904–05	Pat Dougherty	.911	1903–05	Dave Fultz	6
1910–13	Birdie Cree	.969	1919–20	Ping Bodie	8
1939–49	Charlie Keller	.980	1925–33	Earle Combs	22
1949–54	Gene Woodling	**.992	1936–51	Joe DiMaggio	28

Highest Fielding Percentage

1903–05	Dave Fultz	.948
1908–11	Charlie Hemphill	.959
1919–20	Ping Bodie	.964
1922–24	Whitey Witt	.977
1936–51	Joe DiMaggio	.979
1951–68	Mickey Mantle	.983
1965–83	Bobby Murcer	.989

RIGHT FIELD

Most Putouts

1903–09	Willie Keeler	1,148
1920–34	Babe Ruth	3,488

Most Assists

1903–09	Willie Keeler	*90
1920–34	Babe Ruth	150

Most Errors

1903–09	Willie Keeler	*55
1920–34	Babe Ruth	123

Fewest Errors Per Year
(Minimum 5 Years)

1903–09	Willie Keeler	8.8
1937–50	Tommy Henrich	4.1
1948–59	Hank Bauer	3.5
1960–66	Roger Maris	3.3

Most Double Plays

1903–09	Willie Keeler	24
1920–34	Babe Ruth	30

Most Chances Per Game

1903–09	Willie Keeler	1.5
1920–34	Babe Ruth	2.1
1937–50	Tommy Henrich	2.1

Most Total Chances

1903–09	Willie Keeler	1,293
1920–34	Babe Ruth	3,761

Highest Fielding Percentage

1903–09	Willie Keeler	.957
1920–34	Babe Ruth	.967
1937–50	Tommy Henrich	**.983
1948–59	Hank Bauer	.983
1960–66	Roger Maris	*.985

RECORD HOLDERS LIST

1	Jimmy Williams	8
1	Kid Elberfeld	8
1	Wid Conroy	8
1	Willie Keeler	8
1	Joe DiMaggio	8
6	John Ganzel	7
6	Lefty Davis	7
6	Bob Meusel	7
6	Dave Fultz	7
6	Earle Combs	7
6	Red Kleinow	7
6	Roger Peckinpaugh	7
6	Frank Baker	7
6	Babe Ruth	7
15	Joe Dugan	6
15	Bill Dickey	6
15	Pat Dougherty	6
15	Frank Crosetti	6
15	Lou Gehrig	6
20	Charlie Hemphill	5
20	Whitey Witt	5
20	Deacon McGuire	5
20	Ed Sweeney	5
20	Yogi Berra	5
20	Red Rolfe	5
20	Aaron Ward	5
20	Tony Lazzeri	5
28	Mickey Mantle	4
28	Birdie Cree	4
28	Willie Randolph	4
28	Graig Nettles	4
28	Monte Beville	4
33	Ping Bodie	3
33	Charlie Keller	3
33	Bobby Richardson	3
33	Tommy Henrich	3
33	Clete Boyer	3
38	Don Mattingly	2
38	Horace Clarke	2
38	Bill Skowron	2
38	Roger Maris	2
38	Gene Woodling	2
38	Roy White	2
38	Jack O'Connor	2
38	Wally Schang	2
38	Elston Howard	2
38	Phil Rizzuto	2
38	Bucky Dent	2

49	Del Pratt	1	49	Tony Kubek	1
49	Hank Bauer	1	49	Everett Scott	1
49	Eddie Miller	1	49	Andy Carey	1
49	Bobby Murcer	1			

SUMMARY AND HIGHLIGHTS

The outstanding Yankee first basemen have been Hal Chase, Wally Pipp, and Lou Gehrig. While Don Mattingly is primarily known for his bat, he already has won four Golden Gloves.

The Bronx Bombers have had many fine second basemen, beginning with Jimmy Williams, Tony Lazzeri, Joe Gordon, Bobby Richardson, and presently Willie Randolph. Most experts would choose Tony Lazzeri as the best all-around second sacker and offer a toss-up between the fielding abilities of Bobby Richardson and Willie Randolph.

At shortstop Roger Peckinpaugh was the first to earn honorable mention, and it is a very difficult decision selecting the best at this position, because Frank Crosetti, Phil Rizzuto, and Tony Kubek were all excellent all-around performers.

Frank "Home Run" Baker was the first and only Yankee Hall of Famer at third base (the Yankees do not have a shortstop or second baseman in the Hall of Fame), even though they have had such fine players as Joe Dugan, Red Rolfe, and Graig Nettles. Rolfe was the best hitter of this group, but Nettles's combination of power with great range, reflexes, and arm rates him the top all-around third baseman. (He has the most home runs of all Yankee third basemen.)

Bill Dickey and Yogi Berra are easily the greatest Yankee catchers. Berra had more power, but Dickey hit for a higher average. Both were super with the glove, with Dickey being the more graceful. The interesting thing about Yankee catching records is that after Dickey set most of them, he taught Yogi how to catch, and he was such a great teacher (or Yogi was such a great pupil) that Berra went out and broke most of Dickey's catching records!

Thurmon Munson was well on his way to breaking some of these records before his untimely death.

Little-known Birdie Cree was a superstar in left and center fields in the early years of the Yankee franchise. Other exceptional leftfielders were Bob Meusel, Charlie Keller, and Roy White. However, no Yankee leftfielder has yet been voted into the Hall of Fame. Of them, Bob Meusel, a member of Murderers' Row, would seem to have the best chance.

The Yankees have been blessed with three Hall of Famers in center field. Earle Combs was the first, Joe DiMaggio ruled there for 13 years, and when he was done, along came Mickey Mantle. Some people argue over who was the best—Mantle, Duke Snider, or Willie Mays. But if you had to choose between Mantle and DiMaggio, who would you take?

ROGER MARIS
*From 1960 to 1966 he averaged fewer errors than any other
Yankee rightfielder in history. His career 3.3 errors per year
and .985 fielding percentage have not been bettered in 22
years.*

MICKEY MANTLE

Overlooked due to his power hitting is the fact that the Mick averaged the fewest errors of any Yankee centerfielder. His blazing speed enabled him to chase down more fly balls than any other player. Mantle's putout, fewest errors, and total chance marks remain unbroken.

GRAIG NETTLES

No other Yankee third baseman has accumulated as many assists, double plays, or total chances. He was a master with the glove, and he is easily the greatest long-ball hitting third baseman in New York Yankee history.

Graig's 250 round-trippers are 155 more than any other Yankee third baseman.

WILLIE RANDOLPH

Willie has played more games at second base than any other Yankee. Although Tony Lazzeri had more power, many experts will say that Willie Randolph is the better all-around second baseman.

Randolph has the most putouts, assists, DPs, and total chances of any second baseman in New York Yankee history.

Of course there is no problem in right field, where there is no equal to Babe Ruth. But the Bronx Bombers won many pennants and World Series after the Babe because of men like Tommy Henrich, Hank Bauer, Roger Maris, and Reggie Jackson.

It is interesting to note, when baseball fans think of the Babe's bat and not his glove, that Babe Ruth has caught more fly balls and has had more assists, double plays, and total chances than any other rightfielder in New York Yankee history.

CHAPTER X

COMPOSITE
RECORD HOLDERS LISTS

As mentioned before, the Record Holders List does not show players in the order of their greatness. It is a report on the exact number of records established in the season, career, and rookie areas, in batting, pitching, and fielding.

Two separate lists are presented, one for everyday players and one for pitchers.

The records lists show the Yankee pioneer players with more records than some of our great modern players. This is because those players who had the privilege of being the first to wear the Yankee pinstripes were the ones who placed the original records in the book. The early records should not be given a high rating, because of their lack of quality. For example, Tony Lazzeri's 17 records are higher in value than Monte Beville's 36 or Dave Fultz's 43 marks.

It is also important to note that everyone who played after Babe Ruth and Lou Gehrig had a very difficult time in breaking records because they would have had to outdo the two greatest players in New York Yankee history.

This is not to say some of our modern players are not great, but simply that there are varying degrees of greatness.

Hall of Famers such as Joe DiMaggio, Mickey Mantle, and Yogi Berra may not have as many records as others, but the level of their greatness is well known and documented.

DID YOU KNOW that at one time foul balls did not count as strikes? This rule was not changed in the National League until 1901 and the American League until 1903.

When Hugh Duffy set the still-existing season batting-average record of .438, he had an unfair advantage.

EVERYDAY PLAYERS

1	Willie Keeler	*57
1	Jimmy Williams	57
3	Babe Ruth	*56
4	Wally Pipp	52
5	Hal Chase	49
6	Dave Fultz	43
7	Wid Conroy	41
8	Bob Meusel	37
9	Monte Beville	36
10	Roger Peckinpaugh	33
11	Joe DiMaggio	*32
11	Earle Combs	*32
13	Lou Gehrig	*29
13	Kid Elberfeld	29
13	Birdie Cree	29
16	Frank LaPorte	24
17	John Ganzel	18
18	Tony Lazzeri	17
18	Ed Sweeney	17
18	Clyde Engle	17
21	Aaron Ward	16
21	Lefty Davis	16
23	Bill Dickey	*15
23	Frank Baker	*15
23	Guy Zinn	15
26	Neal Ball	14
27	Pat Dougherty	13
27	Deacon McGuire	13
27	Phil Rizzuto	13
27	Jimmy Austin	13
31	Whitey Witt	12
32	Mickey Mantle	*11
32	Yogi Berra	*11
32	Frank Crosetti	11
32	Frank Delahanty	11
36	Charlie Keller	10
36	Charlie Hemphill	10
36	Doc Cook	10
39	Billy Johnson	9

* Hall of Famer

39	Del Pratt	9
39	Roy White	9
39	Luke Boone	9
43	Joe Dugan	8
43	Herm McFarland	8
43	Joe Gordon	8
43	Hack Simmons	8
43	Clete Boyer	8
48	Red Rolfe	7
48	Graig Nettles	7
48	Bobby Richardson	7
48	Tommy Henrich	7
48	George Stirnweiss	7
52	Ray Caldwell	6
52	Harry Wolter	6
52	Hank Bauer	6
52	Danny Hoffman	6
52	Roger Maris	6
52	Elston Howard	6
52	Everett Scott	6
52	Truck Hannah	6
52	Roxy Walters	6
61	Don Mattingly	5
61	Joe Pepitone	5
61	Ira Thomas	5
61	Willie Randolph	5
65	Les Nunamaker	4
65	Bobby Brown	4
65	Ben Chapman	4
65	Ping Bodie	4
65	Fritz Maisel	4
65	Sammy Vick	4
65	Billy Martin	4
65	Johnny Lindell	4
65	Jack O'Conner	4
65	Tom Tresh	4
65	Frank Gilhooley	4
65	Joe Gedeon	4
65	Jerry Coleman	4
65	Muddy Ruel	4
65	Benny Bengough	4

65	Rickey Henderson	4
81	Benny Paschal	3
81	Horace Clarke	3
81	Johnny Sturm	3
81	Mark Koenig	3
81	Roy Hartzell	3
81	Charley Mullen	3
81	Johnny Mize	*3
81	Gil McDougal	3
81	Hugh High	3
81	Steve Whitaker	3
81	Jake Stahl	3
81	Pee Wee Wanninger	3
81	Bert Daniels	3
94	Harvey Hendrick	2
94	John Knight	2
94	Eddie Miller	2
94	Bill Skowron	2
94	Joe Sewell	*2
94	Gene Woodling	2
94	George Selkirk	2
94	Bobby Murcer	2
94	Joe Yeager	2
94	Ray Barker	2
94	Chris Chambliss	2
94	Champ Osteen	2
94	Otis Johnson	2
94	Bob Cerv	2
94	Jack Martin	2
94	Fred Stanley	2
94	Lee Magee	2
94	Sammy Byrd	2
94	John Anderson	2
94	Bucky Dent	2
114	Lynn Lary	1
114	Johnny Blanchard	1
114	Tony Kubek	1
114	Chick Fewster	1
114	Bobby Bonds	1
114	Oscar Grimes	1
114	Walter Blair	1
114	Harry Rice	1
114	Erza Midkiff	1
114	George McQuinn	1
114	Phil Linz	1
114	Johnny Callison	1
114	Jake Powell	1
114	Buddy Hassett	1
114	Earl Gardner	1

PITCHERS

1	Jack Chesbro	*38
2	Clark Griffith	*31
3	Wilcy Moore	26
4	Bob Shawkey	25
5	Johnny Murphy	23
6	Jack Warhop	21
7	Bill Hogg	19
8	Joe Page	18
9	Bill Wolfe	17
10	Sparky Lyle	14
11	Russ Ford	13
12	Red Ruffing	*12
12	Jesse Tannehill	12
14	Whitey Ford	*11
15	Lefty Gomez	*10
16	Ryne Duren	8
16	Rube Manning	8
16	Jake Powell	8
19	Jack Quinn	7
20	Joe Lake	6
21	Luis Arroyo	5
21	Goose Gossage	5
21	Walter Clarkson	5
21	Joe Doyle	5
25	Lindy McDaniel	4
25	Dave Righetti	4
25	Bob Grim	4
28	Ron Guidry	3
28	Dooley Womack	3
28	Waite Hoyt	*3
28	Ray Caldwell	3
28	Bob Keefe	3
28	Tom Sturdivant	3
28	Ambrose Puttman	3
28	Doc Adkins	3
28	Snake Wiltse	3
37	Sam Jones	2
37	George Mogridge	2
37	Pedro Ramos	2
37	Harry Howell	2
37	Thad Tillotson	2
37	Carl Mays	2
37	Spud Chandler	2
37	Al Orth	2
37	Pete Mikkelsen	2
37	Hank Johnson	2
37	Rip Collins	2

37	Ron Davis	2	51	Tommy Byrne	1
37	Brian Fisher	2	51	Lew Brockett	1
37	Herb Pennock	*2	51	Rip Coleman	1
51	King Cole	1	51	Johnny Kucks	1
51	Al Downing	1	51	Atley Donald	1
51	Hippo Vaughn	1	51	Ray Fisher	1
51	Slim Love	1	51	Allan Russell	1
51	Monte Pearson	1	51	Jack Aker	1

CHAPTER XI

MANAGERS SEASON RECORDS

MANAGERS QUIZ

1. Who was the first Yankee manager to have a winning season?
2. Name the Yankee manager who was the first to win more than 100 games.
3. Do you remember the Yankee manager who landed the team in last place for the first time?
4. Which Yankee manager had the highest winning percentage?
5. Who was the Yankee manager who won the pennant by the most games?

DID YOU KNOW that Casey Stengel is the only Major League manager to win five consecutive pennants?

DID YOU KNOW that ten Yankee managers have led their team to a first-place finish? (This is a Major League record.)

DID YOU KNOW that it was 19 years before the Yankees won their first pennant?

Most Wins

1903	Clark Griffith	72
1904	Clark Griffith	92
1920	Miller Huggins	95
1921	Miller Huggins	98
1923	Miller Huggins	98
1927	Miller Huggins	110

Most Losses

1903	Clark Griffith	62
1905	Clark Griffith	78
1907	Clark Griffith	78
1912	Harry Wolverton	102

Highest Winning Percentage

1903	Clark Griffith	.537
1904	Clark Griffith	.609
1920	Miller Huggins	.617
1921	Miller Huggins	.641
1923	Miller Huggins	.645
1927	Miller Huggins	.714

Highest Finish

1903	Clark Griffith	4th
1904	Clark Griffith	2nd
1906	Clark Griffith	2nd
1910	George Stallings	2nd
1921	Miller Huggins	1st
1922	Miller Huggins	1st
1923	Miller Huggins	1st
1926	Miller Huggins	1st
1927	Miller Huggins	1st
1928	Miller Huggins	1st
1932	Joe McCarthy	1st
1936	Joe McCarthy	1st
1937	Joe McCarthy	1st
1938	Joe McCarthy	1st
1939	Joe McCarthy	1st
1941	Joe McCarthy	1st
1942	Joe McCarthy	1st
1943	Joe McCarthy	1st
1947	Bucky Harris	1st
1949	Casey Stengel	1st
1950	Casey Stengel	1st
1951	Casey Stengel	1st
1952	Casey Stengel	1st
1953	Casey Stengel	1st
1955	Casey Stengel	1st
1956	Casey Stengel	1st
1957	Casey Stengel	1st
1958	Casey Stengel	1st
1960	Casey Stengel	1st
1961	Ralph Houk	1st
1962	Ralph Houk	1st
1963	Ralph Houk	1st
1964	Yogi Berra	1st
1976	Billy Martin	1st
1977	Billy Martin	1st
1978	Billy Martin, Dick Howser, and Bob Lemon	1st
1980	Dick Howser	1st
1981	Gene Michael and Bob Lemon	1st

Most Games Won Pennant By

1921	Miller Huggins	4½
1923	Miller Huggins	16
1927	Miller Huggins	19
1936	Joe McCarthy	19½

RECORD HOLDERS LIST

1	Miller Huggins	17
2	Casey Stengel	10
2	Clark Griffith	10
4	Joe McCarthy	9
5	Ralph Houk	3
5	Billy Martin	3
7	Harry Wolverton	1
7	Bucky Harris	1
7	Yogi Berra	1
7	Dick Howser	1
7	Bob Lemon	1

Sandy Amoros on his great catch against Yogi Berra in the 1955 World Series: When asked, "Did you think you had a chance for it?" he replied, "I dunno, I just ran like hell."

Tommy Henrich on Mickey Owen, after Owen's famous passed ball: "He must have felt like a nickel's worth of dog meat."

SUMMARY AND HIGHLIGHTS

Clark Griffith was the very first New York Yankee manager in 1903. Although he did not win a pennant, Griffith had three winning seasons and brought the team in second twice.

Miller Huggins was the first successful manager, and he guided the club to its first pennant, in 1921. It took 19 years for New York to get into the winner's circle, and from that point on they became the greatest team in baseball history.

Huggins had the benefit of Murderers' Row, the famed band of Bronx Bombers that terrorized enemy pitchers. Ruth, Gehrig, Meusel, Lazzeri, and Combs made it a dream for Huggins, who won 110 games in 1927. This represents the most wins by a Yankee team and is considered by most to be the greatest team in the history of the game.

Some would argue that Joe McCarthy's gang of 1936 were better. The 1936 club won the pennant by 19½ games, a half game more than the 1927 team won by.

Joe McCarthy succeeded Huggins and added eight flags to decorate the House that Ruth built. "Marse Joe" won four consecutive titles from 1936 to 1939.

Casey Stengel became the most successful Yankee manager in 1958, when he won his ninth title, and he made it ten in 1960 before bowing out. Casey has the longest consecutive winning streak; from 1949 to 1953 the "Ole Perfessor" won five straight pennants.

Ralph Houk continued in Stengel's footsteps, winning three more in a row from 1961 to 1963. Yogi Berra replaced Houk in 1964 and continued the winning streak.

The Yankees did not win again until Billyball came on in 1976. Billy Martin led them to three straight pennants but received help from Dick Howser and Bob Lemon in the unusual 1978 winning season.

When Casey Stengel took over the reins for the Yankees, it came as a surprise to many baseball people. Casey was an unlikely candidate for the job because in previous managerial stints with the Braves and Dodgers he had finished in the second division nine times out of nine. Casey was somewhat of a clown, and it didn't seem that he fitted into the Yankee tradition. He spoke a garbled—sometimes hardly intelligible—language when he chose, but he could also be shrewd and witty.

Casey was born in Kansas City, Missouri, and his nickname was derived from the city's initials. He became a big leaguer in 1912 and played with the Dodgers, Pirates, Phillies, Giants, and Braves. His most successful years as a player were in 1922 and 1923 with the New York Giants, when as a part-time player he batted .368 and .339. His idol was John McGraw.

Although he did a lot of clowning, Casey took the game of baseball very seriously. He was one of the game's most astute students, observing everything that was going on. He expanded the two-platoon system of baseball. Many managers had used left-handed batters against right-handed pitchers, but Casey was the first to employ this system on a full-time basis. As a result the Yankees won ten pennants and seven World Series under the Ole Perfessor. Moreover, other managers copied Stengel's method of managing, and today the two-platoon system is used by almost all.

George Weiss was running the front office at Yankee Stadium, and it was he who brought Casey to the Bronx. Weiss had always respected Stengel's clear, concise analyses. He knew that Casey could be firm and even severe when it came to demanding business from his players.

JOE McCARTHY

This talented manager took the reins in 1931 and promptly led the club to eight pennants and seven world championships.

McCarthy has the most wins and highest winning percentage in league play, and his 29–9 won-loss record in World Series competition is the best in New York history.

CHAPTER XII

MANAGERS CAREER RECORDS

1. Three men have managed the Yankees for more than ten years. Name them.
2. Who was the first to run the Yankees for more than ten years?
3. Only one manager has been at the helm for more than 2,000 games. Name him.
4. Which manager has the highest winning percentage?
5. Two managers are tied for the most World Series wins. Who are they?

DID YOU KNOW that Miller Huggins won three consecutive pennants twice?

DID YOU KNOW that Joe McCarthy has the highest World Series winning percentage?

DID YOU KNOW that Casey Stengel has won the most pennants, with ten?

Most Years

1903–08	Clark Griffith	6
1918–29	Miller Huggins	12
1931–46	**Joe McCarthy**	**16**

Most Games

1903–08	Clark Griffith	807
1918–29	Miller Huggins	1,796
1931–46	**Joe McCarthy**	**2,347**

Most Wins

1903–08	Clark Griffith	419
1918–29	Miller Huggins	1,067
1931–46	**Joe McCarthy**	**1,460**

Most Losses

1903–08	Clark Griffith	370
1918–29	Miller Huggins	719
1931–46	**Joe McCarthy**	**867**

Highest Winning Percentage

1903–08	Clark Griffith	.520
1918–29	Miller Huggins	.595
1931–46	**Joe McCarthy**	**.627**

Most Pennants

1918–29	Miller Huggins	6
1931–46	Joe McCarthy	8
1949–60	**Casey Stengel**	**10**

Most Consecutive Pennants

1921–23	Miller Huggins	3
1926–28	Miller Huggins	3
1936–39	Joe McCarthy	4
1949–53	**Casey Stengel**	**5**

Most World Series Won

1918–29	Miller Huggins	3
1931–46	Joe McCarthy	7
1949–60	Casey Stengel	7

Most Consecutive Series Won

1918–29	Miller Huggins	2
1931–46	Joe McCarthy	6

Most World Series Games

1918–29	Miller Huggins	33
1931–46	Joe McCarthy	38
1949–60	Casey Stengel	63

Most World Series Games Won

1918–29	Miller Huggins	18
1931–46	Joe McCarthy	29
1949–60	Casey Stengel	37

Most World Series Games Lost

1918–29	Miller Huggins	15
1949–60	Casey Stengel	26

Highest World Series Winning Percentage

1918–29	Miller Huggins	.545
1931–46	**Joe McCarthy**	**.763**

RECORD HOLDERS LIST

1	Miller Huggins	16
2	Joe McCarthy	13
3	Casey Stengel	6
4	Clark Griffith	5

SUMMARY AND HIGHLIGHTS

It is easy to see that Miller Huggins, Joe McCarthy, and Casey Stengel have been the greatest Yankee managers.

Huggins was instrumental in establishing the Yankee dynasty, McCarthy continued the tradition, and Stengel won more pennants than them all.

It has been said the Huggins men were the greatest in pinstripe history, but the record shows that McCarthy's players had the highest winning percentage, and yet Stengel's men won the most pennants.

Miller Huggins began his career as a player with Cincinnati in 1904. As a rookie the little 5' 6½" 140-pounder slammed 129 hits, batted .263, and played a solid second base. His size helped him to lead the league four times in bases on balls, and after playing 6 years with the Reds, he was traded to the Cardinals in 1910. From 1913 to 1916 Huggins was a player-manager, although he only played 18 games in 1916. After 5 years at the helm with two third-place finishes, the fiery little man became the manager of the Yankees in 1918. The Yankees had not yet won their first pennant, and Huggins created improvement year by year until he brought New York their first triumph, in 1921. It was the beginning of the greatest dynasty in baseball. Huggins won three pennants in a row (1921–23) and then duplicated the feat from 1926 to 1928.

The toughest part of Huggins's job was keeping Babe Ruth in line. The two were constantly at each other's throats, and many unpleasantries were exchanged. But the Babe never let his squabbles affect his play.

Who would get your vote for the greatest Yankee manager?

MILLER HUGGINS

This scrappy little manager was 5' 6½" tall and all of 140 pounds. His size did not prevent him from winning six pennants and three World Series.

Huggins had his most outstanding season in 1927 when he won 110 games and lost 44. This winning percentage of .714 is the highest to date.

CASEY STENGEL

The beloved Casey had his own language and ways of doing things, and he knew how to get the job done. He guided the world champions for 12 years, winning ten pennants and seven World Series. His 37 World Series game wins are the most in baseball history.

BIBLIOGRAPHY

Einstein, Charles
The Fireside Book of Baseball
New York: Simon & Schuster, 1987

Carruth, Gorton, and Ehrlich, Eugene
Facts and Dates of American Sports
New York: Harper & Row, 1988

Guinness Sports Record Book
New York: Sterling Publishers, 1988

James, Bill
Bill James Baseball Abstract
New York: Ballantine Books, 1988

James, Bill
Bill James Historical Baseball Abstract
New York: Villard Books, 1986

Microfilms of the New York Times, *1903–1987*
New York: The *New York Times*

Neft, David S., and Cohen, Richard M.
The Baseball Sports Encyclopedia
New York: St. Martin's, 1988

Nelson, Kevin
Baseball's Greatest Quotes
New York: Simon & Schuster, 1982

Reichler, Joseph L.
The Baseball Encyclopedia
New York: Macmillan, 1988

Salant, Nathan
This Date in New York Yankee History
New York: Stein & Day, 1981

Siwoff, Seymour, Hirdt, Steve, and Hirdt, Peter
The Elias Baseball Analyst
New York: Macmillan, 1988

The *Sporting News*
The Complete Baseball Record Book
St. Louis, MO: The Sporting News Publishing Company, 1987

PHOTO CREDITS

I would like to thank the following organizations, individuals, and Major League players who have been so kind as to provide photos for this book:

The National Baseball Hall of Fame and Museum, Inc., Cooperstown, N.Y.

International News, New York

Chris Dunham, Deerfield Beach, Florida

Charles Abatello, Valley Cottage, N.Y.

Phil Rizzuto	Reggie Jackson	Roger Maris
Tommy Henrich	Allie Reynolds	Bobby Shantz
Lou Piniella	Rick Cerone	Charlie Silvera
Johnny Mize	Bill Dickey	Mickey Mantle
Yogi Berra	Bob Turley	Bob Lemon
Gene Woodling	George Selkirk	Joe Dugan

New York Yankee Records

☐ Endless delight for fans of baseball and the legendary Bronx bombers.

* Who led the Yankees in wins, E.R.A. and strikeouts in the year of your birth?

* What nine Yankee rookie records are held by Joe DiMaggio?

* Who played more seasons for the Yankees: Mickey Mantle, Lou Gehrig or Yogi Berra?

* Which Yankees performed the best during World Series, playoffs and All-Star games?

* Can you name the Yankee batting stars who also led in fielding percentage, most putouts and double plays?

All the answers are in this book, along with rare photographs, player profiles and full stats.

A superb gift for the legions of sports fans.

(ISBN 1-56171-215-9)

To order in North America, please sent this coupon to: **S.P.I. Books** •136 W 22nd St. • New York, NY 10011 • Tel: 212/633-2022 • Fax: 212/633-2123

Please send European orders with £ payment to:
Bookpoint Ltd. • 39 Milton Park • Abingdon Oxon OX14 4TD • England • Tel: (0235) 8335001 • Fax: (0235) 861038

Please send ___ books. I have enclosed check or money order for $4.99 U.S./£3.50 ST.____ (please add $1.95 U.S./£ for first book for postage/handling & 50¢/50p. for each additional book). Make dollar checks drawn on U.S. branches payable to **S.P.I. Books**; Sterling checks to **Bookpoint Ltd**. Allow 2 to 3 weeks for delivery.

___ MC ___ Visa # _____

Exp. date _____

Name _____

Address _____

New S.P.I. Bestselling Baseball Books

A Day In the Season of the L.A. Dodgers

☐ All baseball lovers, and especially Dodger fans, will delight in this intimate visit to Dodger Stadium. There are photographs, interviews and descriptions of all the people and places that turn on the magic at this premier big league ballpark.

The reader not only meets big name baseball personalities like manager Tommy Lasorda and stars like Darryl Strawberry and Orel Hersheiser, but also fans, announcers, grounds crew and concession salespeople.

We meet both the guy who throws peanut bags in the stands and the one who throws curveballs in batting practice. Even a season ticket holder will have plenty to learn and love in this ode to the American pastime.

(ISBN 1-56171-084-9)

Babe Ruth's Incredible Records and the Forty-Five Players Who Broke Them

❑ No one changed baseball's record book like Babe Ruth.

Some of the Babe's incredible career records will probably stand forever, while many of his single season records were recently topped by modern era greats.

What do you know about these record-breakers and the man whose slugging standard they all tried to match?

* Has anyone knocked in more RBI's than Ruth in a season? In a career?

* Which players came closest to the Babe's career home run mark before Hank Aaron?

* What are Ruth's longstanding fielding and strikeout records?

* Did anyone break the Babe's mark for homeruns by a pitcher?

The answers to all these and much more are found in this unique treasure trove (packed with photos) for every baseball fan.

(ISBN 1-56171-221-3)

To order in North America, please sent this coupon to: **S.P.I. Books** •136 W 22nd St. • New York, NY 10011 • Tel: 212/633-2022 • Fax: 212/633-2123

Please send European orders with £ payment to:
Bookpoint Ltd. • 39 Milton Park • Abingdon Oxon OX14 4TD • England • Tel: (0235) 8335001 • Fax: (0235) 861038

Please send ____ books. I have enclosed check or money order for $5.50 U.S./£3.50 ST.____ (please add $1.95 U.S./£ for first book for postage/handling & 50¢/50p. for each additional book). Make dollar checks drawn on U.S. branches payable to **S.P.I. Books**; Sterling checks to **Bookpoint Ltd**. Allow 2 to 3 weeks for delivery.

___MC ___ Visa # _____
Exp. date _____
Name _____
Address _____

Official Profiles of Baseball Hall of Famers

❏ All of baseball's greatest hitters, pitchers, fielders, rookies and managers are
profiled in this one-of-a-kind new book. You not only get their season-by-
season and total career records, you even get their birthdays and nicknames.

Want to ask or answer some tough trivia questions about Hall of Fame pitchers
like Lefty Groove, Don Drysdale or Whitey Ford? Do you want to compare the
home run records of Hank Aaron, Babe Ruth and Harmon Killebrew? The
answeres are all here.

Perhaps you want to see what chance your favorite player has of getting into the
Hall of Fame. Now you can easily compare Roger Clemens' strikeout records to
those of Koufax. Stack up Cecil Fielder's slugging percentage against Stan
Musial, and see if Ozzie Smith's fielding records put him on a par with Brooks
Robinson.

Guarantees endless fascination for the baseball fan.

(ISBN 1-56171-216-7)

To order in North America, please sent this coupon to: **S.P.I. Books** •136 W 22nd St. • New York, NY 10011 •
Tel: 212/633-2022 • Fax: 212/633-2123

Please send European orders with £ payment to:
Bookpoint Ltd. • 39 Milton Park • Abingdon Oxon OX14 4TD • England • Tel: (0235) 8335001 • Fax: (0235) 861038

Please send____books. I have enclosed check or money order for $10.99 U.S./£6.99 ST.____(please add $1.95 U.S./£ for
first book for postage/handling & 50¢/50p. for each additional book). Make dollar checks drawn on U.S. branches payable to
S.P.I. Books; Sterling checks to **Bookpoint Ltd**. Allow 2 to 3 weeks for delivery.
___MC ___ Visa # _____
Exp. date _____
Name _____
Address _____